Jasmine's Revenge
Tooley Times 2

(Chapter Titles)

Chapter 1: Love/Hate
Chapter 2: Dark Past
Chapter 3: The Old Me
Chapter 4: The Love Child
Chapter 5: Plan of Revenge
Chapter 6: Blank Tombstones
Chapter 7: Tooley's Hair & Nails
Chapter 8: A Shot at Love
Chapter 9: Best Served Cold
Chapter 10: Closeted
Chapter 11: Weak Wives
Chapter 12: Third Time's the Charm
Chapter 13: Pure Luck
Chapter 14: Kill or Be Killed
Chapter 15: Us against the World
Chapter 16: The Return of Michael Yancy
Chapter 17: The Return of an Old Friend
Chapter 18: Over My Dead Body Part 1
Chapter 19: Deranged
Chapter 20: Over My Dead Body Part 2
Chapter 21: Britney's Revenge
Chapter 22: Angel of Mine
Chapter 23: Serendipity

Firstly—*as always*—I'd like to thank my Lord and Savior Jesus Christ. Secondly, I dedicate this book to my mother (Helen) and my husband (Joe)… and last *but certainly not least,* THANK YOU! (Yes YOU… *whoever you are*) for supporting my craft and constantly reading the drama I create on paper.
Follow me on Instagram and let me know your thoughts on any or all of my work: **@WeirdGirlWrites**
Also, be sure to like "**A Tangier Tale Publishing**" on Facebook. Thank you in advance for your continuous support… and enjoy!
☺

i

Chapter 1: Love/Hate

~Present Day 2016~

Calvin's head is leaned all the way back against the headboard and his eyes are squeezed shut. He's lying naked, comfortably; spread out across our king sized bed enjoying his morning surprise. His hand is on the back of my head pushing my mouth further down onto his fully erect penis. I woke him up with my tongue dancing along the shaft of his dick this morning.

"Yea baby just like that." He moans as I begin to do some new, intricate tricks with my jaws. I haven't given him head like this in a while, but I figured since it was his birthday—why not? I hungrily continue to French kiss from the tip of his dick to its base. It's visibly driving him crazy. I can always tell when Calvin is about to cum when his left leg starts to shake uncontrollably and he, sort of, holds his breath. Finally, after about twenty minutes, I feel him explode into my mouth and I make sure to lick up and swallow every last drop. "Damn, baby." He lets out a loud sigh of relief, "I really needed that shit, what a great way to start my birthday." He laughs.

"No problem, baby." I respond nonchalantly and then I get up and race to the bathroom. In the heat of the moment, sucking and swallowing cum sounds great and exciting… but after the adrenaline wears off, if I don't brush my teeth right away and gargle extensively with mouthwash, I end up feeling terrifically nauseous. Plus, I haven't swallowed cum in a while—at least not his.

I've known Calvin Duggar for over sixteen years now, well technically longer than that, but the first time we ever met face to face was in the year 2000. Calvin is one of the most legendary rap artists of our time… you may know him better by his stage name; Homeboy Duggar. In the prime of his career *(from 1993-2005)* Calvin was the biggest star in the country and every woman wanted to be by his side, but now that the smoke has cleared and his fame has subsided—that's no longer the case. I'm literally all Mr. Duggar really has left in the world. Don't get me wrong, he's still a very attractive man: six feet tall, dark flawless skin, long rock-star hair, fairly muscular, and even though he's four years away from fifty, he still has the fashion sense of a young hipster (*all without trying too hard or looking creepy in the process*)—but we all know none of that matters because groupies only chase money. Throughout the years I've watched all the screaming female fans dwindle, even his entourage of 'yes men' went ghost. Groupies definitely have ZERO interest in looking after a cripple who is one remark away from a full blown mid-life crisis, luckily for him I was never in it for the money or fame.

"Damn how long are you going to be in the damn bathroom, Jasmine? I have to pee!" I hear him scream from the bedroom.

"Shut the hell up! I'm almost done, asshole!" I yell back. This was our everyday dialogue.

After brushing my teeth and tongue for over fifteen minutes, I finally exit the bathroom to find Calvin on crutches limping past me and giving me a good shove before entering the bathroom and closing the door in my face. "Asshole!" I murmur once more, this time under my breath… Not that I gave a damn about whether or not he heard me. Getting over our mini spat, I make my way to the kitchen and begin to fix him a nice big birthday breakfast.

If on the day Duggar and I met (back in 2000), someone would've came to me and told me that he and I would end up domestic partners, I would've called bullshit. Yet here we are, sixteen years since our initial assembly, playing house like the dysfunctional masochists that we are. Do I love the man? Yes. I would give my life for Calvin. We have an unhealthy, yet strangely unbreakable, bond. Am I happy? Not necessarily, but I've been worse off in my lifetime, so this emotionally abusive situation is a walk in the park compared to my past physically abusive ones.

Although our arguments sometimes get out of hand, Calvin has never laid a hand on me. He grew up in an abusive household himself and he's even beaten on other women that he was previously in relationships with… but till this very day he has never caused me any bodily harm. He always tells me he'd beat himself to a pulp before he ever touched me, and I believe him wholeheartedly. I can see he has a soft side when it comes to me and I love that about him. Deep down I can tell he appreciates everything I've done and continue to do for him. "Your breakfast is on the table!" I yell to him from the kitchen. I then place the eggs, bacon, waffles, and hash browns I have prepared for him at his regular seating place at the head of the kitchen table. It is truly a breakfast fit for a king... *my* king.

"Smells amazing!" He limps over to me. "Thank you, love." He says as he leans in and kisses me softly on my forehead.

"Anything for you, baby. Happy birthday!" I smile.

"God, I'm getting old." He says gloomily, only halfway playing. I know for a fact that getting older is a scary thought for someone who once considered himself a god. I just recently turned thirty-seven myself, so I can kind of relate; thirty-seven might as well be fifty in *female-stripper* years.

"Nah, never that, you don't look a day over twenty-one." I reassure him. I wasn't lying; Calvin looked GREAT for his age. If I didn't know him inside and out, I would assume he was in his early thirties at MOST.

"You're right; after my leg heals I'm going to be right back on that big stage." He mutters.

"Yea, baby... Sure." I appease his ego, but we both knew Calvin would never perform on a stage again. Simply walking from the bedroom to the kitchen causes him excruciating pain, so I doubt he'll be able to jump up and down from stage left to stage right like he used to.

Calvin was shot in his left shin ten years ago, he wasn't even supposed to ever walk again, but miraculously after years of physical therapy he took his first steps without crutches recently. It takes him hours to get from point A to point B, plus bones heal slower when you're older and he just turned forty-six years old today, so yea—he needs to finally let that rap star, pipe dream go.

~Flashback 1997~

A year after I first moved *(or fled)* to Dumois, Missouri at age seventeen, I became a HUGE fan of Mr. Calvin Duggar thanks to my then roommate, Dixie. Dixie had every single album of Duggar's and most of his posters were plastered all over her bedroom wall. I met Dixie when I started working at a run-down strip club, we were both rookie dancers at the time and I was tired of living at bus stops and sometimes in motel rooms so she allowed me to move into her house. She was enrolled in a low income housing program so we were able to live there for only forty dollars a month.

After months of putting our money together we were able to acquire tickets to a Homeboy Duggar concert shortly after I moved in with her. I grew up dirt poor in Chicago where nobody around me was spending money on luxuries like concerts or music, money in the households I was raised in was solely spent on drugs, alcohol, clothing, food, guns, and/or bills. I had what I can only describe as a divine awakening at that first Duggar concert. I fell in love with both hip hop and him that very day.

    I remember that night like it was yesterday, even though we paid close to a hundred dollars for each ticket, we still managed to have horrible seats. Despite the atrocious placement, I became captivated by the amazing music and experience. I was astonished by how the entire crowd became completely enamored by Duggar's routine. That night he was nothing short of remarkable. I related to the subject matter of almost every song he performed, it honestly felt like he was rapping directly out of pages from my diary. After that night I immediately fell in love with him as an artist and even more so as a man. I heard the vulnerability and honesty in his voice and it turned my feelings for him from that of an innocent fanatic to an obsessed addict—from that point on (in my head of course), Duggar became my man. So imagine how sick with envy I became when towards the end of that show I witnessed Calvin pull up three screaming admirers (who were initially seated in the front row) on to the stage.

    "If we had better seats that could have been us, we look way better than those girls!" I spat at Dixie.

    "Girl, please! You didn't even really want to come tonight, let alone spend the hundred dollars on these crappy seats! So I know damn well if I told you about the six hundred dollar increase it would take to upgrade to those front row seats you wouldn't even have heard me out!" She yelled back at me. She was right, but now that I had seen Duggar live and heard firsthand how beautiful his music was, I vowed that the next time he was in town I would be front row, center. I looked on at the jumbo screen as the three lucky female fans he pulled on stage began to grind and twerk on him and his entourage.

    One day that'll be me, I thought to myself.

~Fast forward three years later to the year 2000~

I was twenty-one, I landed a job working as an assistant legal secretary at one of the biggest law firms in North America, and I was able to finally afford front row Duggar tickets. So visualize my distraught when every single Duggar ticket sold out within the first hour of them being on sale. Fortunately, I was, and still am, a persistent and driven woman; no one was going to tell me that after finally being in a good place in my life that I *still* wouldn't be able to see my favorite artist up close and personal. So I had to pull some major strings because sold out or not, I was going to go to that damn concert.

I remember immediately logging into a random local AOL chat room and typing [ANYONE HAVE FRONTROW HOMEBOY DUGGAR TICKETS FOR HIS SHOW IN DUMOIS NEXT MONTH?] under the username: DuggarFan79. Initially I didn't get any responses, except from the usual online trolls that hid safely behind their computers.

[NO ONE HAS THOSE DAMN TICKETS YOU IDIOT, ESPECIALLY NOT FRONT ROW] one troll rudely responded back to me.

Ignoring them I kept being persistent. [I AM A 21/f/MO, I'm GREAT LOOKING, and I will fuck and suck any guy *(or girl)* who can get me front row tickets to that sold out Homeboy Duggar concert in Tooley!] And just like that hundreds of people in the chat room were responding to me, I guess the saying was true; sex *definitely* sells. I skimmed through about a thousand fake trolls who I knew didn't really have the tickets, but were only mentioning me because I had posted some extremely freaky shit. After a couple of hours of skimming, I ended up narrowing down my search to an eighteen-year-old rich kid from Uptown Tooley.

[EddieTheCoolGuy (6:48pm): Send me a picture!]

[DuggarFan79 (6:48pm): Nice try… Send me a pic of the tickets first.]

[EddieTheCoolGuy (6:50pm): Nope! My tickets, my rules!]

[DuggarFan79 (6:51pm): … K.] I gave in and sent him a picture of me in a very risky and revealing outfit.

[EddieTheCoolGuy (6:55pm): Dammmmmn girl!] He finally responded. He was right to say damn. I was and still am very a beautiful specimen. I am petite, but thick, I have fair skin, I have a huge round ass that you can see from the front, and I also have a big, thick, curly head of hair equipped with light brown streaks that I was born with. In the particular picture I sent him that night, I was wearing my favorite stripper outfit that I used to rock back when I was a dancer. He fell for the bait and he fell hard—mind you I was getting all this attention way before I ever enhanced my breasts, which ended up happening years later.

[EddieTheCoolGuy (6:56pm): Girl you can HAVE my tickets, but you got to promise to let me see that body in person] He said eagerly.

[DuggarFan79 (6:56): That's fine.] I replied, excited that my AOL chat room plan had actually worked.

[EddieTheCoolGuy (6:57pm): So… when do you want to meet up?]

[DuggarFan79 (6:57): Tonight.] I said and then gave him my cell phone number.

[EddieTheCoolGuy (6:58pm): That's actually perfect because my parents aren't expected home until really late. Just hurry up and get here!] He informed me. So that same night I ended up catching like three buses to get to him (because at the time I didn't drive). This was around the time the Dumois/Tooley divide was starting to become more noticeable.

-You see, Tooley used to be a part of Dumois, but in the early nineties the government began to gentrify the area. They basically split the city in half and divided the upper class from the lower class citizens by train tracks. The newly gentrified/refurbished area was renamed Tooley and the further away from original Dumois and west of the train tracks you went, the more expensive and high class the area became. -

So that day I took a two-hour bus from the low income housing area of Dumois I lived in, to the most expensive neighborhood in Tooley where that eighteen-year-old kid, Eddie, was waiting for me at the door of his mansion.

"Hi." He said almost star struck. "Thank God you're real; I thought you were going to look completely different than your picture." He said sounding relieved. "You actually look ten times better!"

"Thank you… I don't have time to play around online tricking people; I've had my heart set on those tickets for a very long time." I responded honestly. "Are you going to invite me in or not?" I egged on, eager to do what I needed to do to get the damn tickets and head back home. It was already almost nine thirty at night.

"Okay… My parents will be home at like midnight, they're at a dinner now so we have to hurry." *Hurry? I remember thinking; this kid won't last five minutes with me, let alone two and a half hours.* Nonetheless, he took my hand and rushed me into his enormous house. Once inside I realized the outside didn't do it any justice, it was absolutely beautiful. Coming from poverty in Chicago to poverty in Dumois, I had never really seen the inside of a luxurious home in my entire life—*except on TV of course*. This kid had absolutely no idea how good he had it. The old, Chicago 'me' would have tied Eddy up and rummaged through his home for almost everything I could actually carry with me onto public transportation… but that was the old me.

After walking up what felt like an eternity of steps, we arrived on the floor his bedroom was on. "Where are the tickets?" I demanded, still a little skeptical even though he sent me plenty of pictures holding the tickets to reassure me.

"Damn, straight to the point." He laughed. "I like you… Here." He handed me an envelope he had just retrieved from his back pocket. I opened up the envelope and there they were; two front row tickets to the sold out Homeboy Duggar concert. I was IMMEDIATELY turned on. As soon as I tucked the tickets safely into a side pocket of my bag, I removed my trench coat revealing the exact same outfit I wore in the picture I had sent him earlier. "Damn, damn, damn." The boy chanted. *Damn, damn, damn* was right. I was going to give this kid the business! I had begun assuming the position and getting down on my knees when my conscience kicked in.

"Wait… let me see your ID to make sure you're actually eighteen years old before I get started." I demanded, catching him off guard.

"ID?" I remember him looking puzzled.

"Well I'm not about to have sex with a minor." I barked.

"You didn't say that before, we never talked about verifying my age. And who cares anyways, why does it matter? I won't tell anyone." He insisted.

"I care." I coldly replied. I had my very own personal experiences, limits, and reasons for not wanting to partake in the *raping* of a minor even if it is consensual and means giving up my front row Duggar tickets.

"I don't have an ID." He immediately looked defeated.

"Well I can't fuck or suck you." I stood firmly in my beliefs. I wanted those tickets badly, but not at *any* cost. I began to gloomily reach back into my bag and pull out the tickets to hand them back to the boy.

"No, keep them." He sighed. "Truth is I'm only seventeen and a virgin and I wouldn't even know what to do with a body like yours anyways." He admitted. "I'm just glad I got to see who I saw in the picture online—in person. Besides, I'm not even that big of a Homeboy Duggar fan anyways. I only got my parents to buy the tickets to impress my friends at school." He shared. Ecstatic, I ran towards Eddie and embraced him.

"Thank you." I said kissing him on his cheek. He hugged me tight and I felt his under aged dick growing from inside his pants. I suddenly became uncomfortable again. "Okay boy, that's enough." I said disgusted and in a rush. "BYE!"

"I'm so sorry, you're just so beautiful." He responded slightly embarrassed.

"It's okay." I smiled at him one last time before basically sprinting out of his house and heading back to my little crappy life.

A month after that I ended up taking my then supervisor, Britney Greene, with me to the show. I didn't have the money to buy her a birthday present because she was an uppity rich bitch who lived in Tooley, so I figured giving her those front row tickets would impress her. Turned out her wack-ass was indifferent about them, she barely even heard of Duggar and knew NOTHING about his music. Dixie still hasn't forgiven me for choosing to take Britney over her 'til this day, but at the time I was trying to get in Britney's good graces. After all, she would always buy me lunch at work, give me rides home, and even let me practice driving in her Mercedes—the tickets were the least I could do.

I remember the concert was on a Wednesday night and I had to basically beg her to go since it was a work night. She acted extremely fake to me now that I look back on everything. I mean, when I first started working at the firm, she told me all her past hoe-stories and I thought we had the *realness* aspect in common. Unfortunately, that wasn't the case at all; she turned out to be one of those former hoes who began to think they were holier than thou now that they'd found Jesus. I had to force her to wear a sexy white dress to the concert that accentuated her equally beautiful body. To her this was just a stupid concert, to me… It was what I waited three years of my life for.

Anyways the both of us looked sexy enough in our white skimpy dresses to one up the three fanatics I had seen go on stage with Duggar three years earlier. Britney and I actually earned access to meet Duggar and his crew after the concert was over. I already had it in my head for three years straight that if I had ever met Homeboy Duggar I would do whatever it took for him to gain interest in me and never forget our encounter. Britney didn't know how deeply infatuated I was with Calvin, and ended up calling me thirsty almost a hundred times that night even though she slept with almost all of the guys in our city. Ignoring her, I remember getting down and dirty that night. I don't remember much about it because I was so high and drunk, but I do remember being involved in an orgy with Duggar and his crew. I also remember the heartbreak I endured at the end of it all.

"Can I call you sometime?" I called after Calvin as he began to put his clothes back on and head out almost immediately after we finished having sex.

"Girl, bye." He laughed at me as him and his boys left the building. I remember feeling so defeated and used that night. I wish I had a real friend to lean on in my weakest moment, but I didn't. Britney just looked at me like I was a dirty disappointment and Dixie was still livid at me for choosing to go with Britney instead of her. I had no one to talk to and my soul was honestly crushed. Having sex with Calvin for the first time happened nothing like I imagined it would. I wanted him to fall in love with me but instead I became just another groupie to him. For three years I thought Calvin was the love of my life, I thought we would've connected through music, so the fact that he carried me after it all went down was a blow I felt in my spirit. If I was a weak bitch I would have taken my life that night, but I've never been one, so I endured it all. I just looked at my *friend* differently after that, and I'm pretty sure the lost trust was mutual. Taking that fake ass hoe with me to that concert was one of the biggest mistakes I have ever made; Dixie would have had my back, understood me, and would never have acted as bougie as Britney did that night.

    Anyways, that was the beginning of my history with Calvin Duggar. Luckily for me, the next time we met was quite different… And it always amazes me how we came from that groupie/celebrity relationship, to this love/hate relationship we have today. Despite it all, I honestly can't see myself living a life without Duggar and I know deep down he feels the same way about me.

Chapter 2: Dark Past

~Present Day 2016~

I am watching Calvin from the kitchen, he's laid out on the living room couch, half asleep, stomach full from the breakfast I prepared for him and his body looks extremely relaxed from the head I had administered to him earlier. Our relationship is very unique, I'm here because I feel like I owe him my life, and he's here because he feels like currently, I AM his entire life. After all, I'm the reason the former rap sensation Homeboy Duggar was shot to begin with. He lost his career by saving my life. So regardless of how dysfunctional we are together, he will always be my hero. Despite how pathetic he seems right now; jobless, broke, out of shape, disgruntled, bitter, mean, etc.—I owe him more than I could ever repay him. We also come from a very similar background of abuse. As children we encountered a lot of adversity, so that empathetic bond in itself created a soft place in my heart for him. I also think more than anything, opening up to one another about everything we've ever faced in our past is what has cemented our unfounded love for almost ten years. Calvin has shared some sick moments from his adolescence with me, stuff I know for a fact he has never told another living soul.

~Flashback 1978~

Calvin Duggar was really young when he first encountered sexual abuse. Son of a drug dealing father and a drug addicted mother; you'd think they'd be the ones to corrupt his innocence… But that wasn't the case at all. Yes, having flawed parents probably impacted a lot of the way he ended up viewing the world, but in his parents' defense, regardless of both their issues, they were always able to provide for, and shelter their son—that is, until he turned eight.

Duggar grew up in Dumois but hardly ever admits it. When asked in interviews where he was born and raised, he vaguely responds "Missouri". I don't blame him. It's hard for me to associate with the streets of Chicago because of all the horrible things that happened to me growing up there, so I understand him wanting to distance himself from his past. He still always gave back to his hometown when he was on top, and throughout his career he always made sure to perform a majority of his shows at arenas located in nearby Tooley.

    Anyways, getting back to the tragedy that occurred late 1978 (Calvin remembers every detail of the event); an eight-year-old Duggar was outside at a park about three blocks from his home. His parents were always in the streets but made sure he had enough money and food for weeks on end. His parents weren't concerned about someone kidnapping their son or trying anything because Calvin's father was at the top of the food pyramid in his neighborhood. If anyone so much as laid a hand on Mr. Duggar's only son, there would be unfathomable blood shed throughout the streets. Plus, the Duggar's gave back to their community so much so; they were more revered than despised.

    "Aren't you KB's son?" An older boy about fourteen or fifteen said while approaching Calvin who was innocently playing on the playground's swing set.

    "Yes." Calvin nodded.

    "Your pops is a legend; I want to be just like him." The older boy continued. Of course the young eight-year-old Duggar was used to this sort of attention. Even grown men in their forties would kiss Calvin's ass in hopes of it getting them in a closer relationship with his father. Calvin didn't grasp the altitude of the power his family possessed, he just knew during Christmas and his birthdays he would always receive more gifts than any child in his entire state.

    "Yea I know." He responded nonchalantly.

    "I bet you have all the cool toys." The boy continued enviously.

    "I just got that Coleco Telstar Marksman." Calvin bragged as an eight-year-old boy would.

    "WHAT? Man you're lying." The boy replied cunningly.

    "Nuh unh! I really do!" Calvin said annoyed.

    "Man, that system JUST came out this year." The teenager continued to antagonize him.

    "I know! And my daddy got it for me." Duggar whined; a little annoyed that someone would dare question him.

    "Prove it." The devious teen kept on.

"Okay, follow me." Calvin said hopping off the swing. He began walking towards his house on Hampton Avenue. At the time Hampton Avenue was one of the only streets in Dumois that wasn't part of government housing. The teenage boy looked around suspiciously to ensure nobody saw him following Calvin into his house. He clearly had bad intentions in mind but Calvin was too young to pick up on anything.

"Wow, y'all crib is hooked up." The teen gawked at how exquisitely decorated the inside of the house was. "I wouldn't even know this is how nice the inside was looking from the outside." He gasped. He was right to be amazed. From the outside, the Duggar household appeared to be a basic three story town home; whereas on the inside, the décor looked expensive and modern.

"Yea, it's okay… But DON'T TELL ANYONE you've been in here. My pops doesn't like people in my house... I could get in big trouble." Calvin wasn't lying, the last time he let people in his house before running it by his father he got his first ass whooping. His parents were always afraid of crack fiends or undercover policemen getting into their home to either steal from them or search the premises without a warrant to find evidence— either instance would be bad for business and could potentially bring down Mr. Duggar's entire operation.

"I won't, I won't. Listen, I don't want to get killed by your father either, my lips are sealed." The teen reassured Calvin. "Now where's this game you claim you have?"

"I got it, I got it. It's upstairs in my room." Calvin barked and led the teen up the flight of stairs into his Batman themed bedroom. The stranger then locked the bedroom door behind them.

"When are your parent's coming home?" He asked.

"Not for another two hours." Calvin said while hooking up the game system.

"Okay good." The boy smirked. The two began to play the game for about half an hour when the teen got restless. "I'm getting bored." He said out of nowhere.

"WHAT? This is Coleco Telstar Marksman, NO ONE ELSE HAS THIS you CAN'T be bored." Calvin laughed in disbelief at the older boy's statement.

"You're right, but maybe I just want to play something else." He hungrily looked Calvin up and down.

"Like what?" A naïve, yet uncomfortable Calvin questioned. That's when the boy slowly began to unzip his jeans.

"You ever seen someone else's dick before?" the teen chuckled as he reached for his member.

"Ew, that's disgusting." Calvin shrieked.

"It's only disgusting if you're a big baby." The boy egged on. "You're not a big baby are you?"

"I'M NOT A BABY!" Calvin spat.

"Okay, okay…. You're not a baby." The teen mocked. "You know how you can prove to me you're not a baby?" He continued.

"How?" Calvin asked curiously.

"You can look at my dick and touch it for me." The boy said while finally exposing his fully erect penis.

"YUCK!" Calvin jumped back. "Put that away now, that's disgusting!" He yelled getting up and making his way to his bedroom door.

"Just come here and touch it, it's really not that bad." The boy insisted.

"This can't be right. This doesn't feel right. You need to get out of my house before I tell my father." Calvin threatened.

"YEA RIGHT, like YOU'RE going to tell KB-the-god that YOU let some stranger kid in his house without permission? You're a damn liar!" The boy chuckled. "Now come over here and suck my dick before I tell on YOU."

"You would tell my parents I had you in here?" Calvin asked frightened at the thought.

"Hell yea! I would tell them you dragged me in here and wanted to show me where your dad hid all of his drugs and money."

"I DID NOT!" Calvin yelled.

"I know, but I'll lie." The teenager smirked.

"Please don't tell my dad!" Calvin is close to tears.

"Okay, okay you cry baby. Just come over here and touch it and I'll go home and your parents will never find out that I'd ever been in here." He relentlessly bargained.

"You promise?" Calvin asked whimpering.

"Yea... I swear." The boy said while he completely undressed and laid down, spread-eagle style on Calvin's bed. A disgusted young Duggar solemnly approached the teen, sat beside his naked body on the bed, closed his eyes and reached for the teen's dick. In less than a split second the teen went ballistic and grabbed the back of Calvin's head, shoving his entire face into his exposed crotch area. "OPEN YOUR DAMN MOUTH!" The older boy screamed, "OPEN YOUR FUCKING MOUTH!" He began to squeeze and apply pressure on the back of the eight-year-old's neck.

"OUCH!" Calvin opened his mouth to scream in pain, only to have the teenager shove his penis deep in the depths of Calvin's innocent mouth. Calvin fought back and immediately bit down hard on the teen's dick while simultaneously punching the older boy on his sides.

"FUCK!" The teen boy cried out while grabbing his penis in pain and rolling onto the floor. Calvin took that opportunity to run into his father's bedroom and grab the gun Mr. Duggar kept underneath his mattress. He raced back to his own bedroom and pointed the gun at the still whaling teen.

"Get your clothes and GET THE FUCK OUT OF MY HOUSE!" Calvin screamed as tears streamed down his face.

"Please, please, I'm sorry. Don't shoot, I'm sorry." The boy pleaded.

"NOW!" Calvin screamed while cocking the gun and aiming it directly over the teens already sore penis. "GET OUT OF MY HOUSE! And if I ever see you again, I'LL KILL YOU!" Seeing the seriousness in Calvin's face caused the teen to grab his clothes and sprint out of the Duggar household before he even had the opportunity to get dressed. Calvin watched in tears as the stranger raced down the street naked. He never saw that boy again; but on that day his innocence was stolen forever.

~Present Day 2016~

I randomly throw up while lying on the couch next to Duggar. "MAN! What the FUCK, Jasmine?" He yells while sitting up.

"I don't know what happened, I just felt really nauseous all of a sudden." I get up and go to the kitchen to wet a dish rag I plan on using to clean up my mess.

"You're either pregnant or on drugs." Duggar says accusingly.

"FUCK YOU! I don't do drugs, FOOL!" I scoff.

"Sure you don't…" Duggar says skeptically, "…then you must be fucking other men if you're pregnant because it sure as hell isn't mine! I thought you were going to go to the doctor?" This is the second time this week I have randomly gotten sick in front of Calvin. I did say a couple of days ago I would go see a doctor or take a pregnancy test but I've been too scared to face reality and do either. Duggar is right, if I am pregnant, it isn't his. Duggar and I have been having unprotected sex for the past ten years, he's cum in me each and every instance… And I have never ONCE gotten pregnant—neither have the millions of groupies he once had lined up at his fingertips. This baby, *if I am in fact pregnant*, is definitely not his. "Since you're out here fucking around I'm going to tell Miya to come scoop me and stay at her place for the night." I cringe at his words. It's been almost a year since I heard that name come out of his mouth.

I fucking hate Miya; Miya is one of Duggar's former groupies that can't seem to let him go — even now after the fame surrounding him has subsided. She used to swear she was my competition back in the day. I've never actually seen her, just heard about her a lot from Duggar and their sexual relationship irks me. Whenever he and I have ever had a disagreement he would always wobble his ass out of here and go stay with her. Don't get me wrong, I'm not at all intimidated by what they have going on; it just comes off as disrespectful to me, but I really can't fight it too much, because after all… I currently might be pregnant with someone else's child. I have no right to be upset by my boyfriend's infidelity when currently *unfaithfulness* is my middle name.

"Do you. Just make sure you're home by midnight or I'm locking you out of this house." I lash out at him. "And wear a freakin' condom, because I don't want to catch anything." Even though our relationship is fairly open, at the end of the day he knows damn well to whom he belongs—he also knows whose name is on the mortgage. Mystery Miya is also lucky that she's never been introduced to the old me... because *the old me* would have already put a bullet through her temple.

Chapter 3: The Old Me

~Flashback 1979-1993~

 The old me is a thorough killer. The old me has killed three times and has never felt any remorse or regret for my actions. It is my belief that a killer is made; not born.

 My name is Jasmine Hall and I was born in Chicago on May 23rd 1979 to Cyrus Vermont Hall III and Eva Maxine Brown-Hall. My parents were the epitome of what parents should be and way more responsible than Calvin's parents. I wasn't spoiled or hood rich, in fact, I was the complete opposite of that—but I was always given the basic necessities and resources needed to lead a humble, yet decent life. I remember being an extremely happy child. My mother worked at a local women's shelter for little to nothing, and my father was a janitor at Moses Montefiore Public School. They weren't the wealthiest people when it came to money, but they were extremely wealthy in love and happiness. They wanted the very best for me; their only child. A majority of all the money they'd ever earned was put aside and saved in hopes of one day being able to move our family out of Chicago to somewhere safer. Unfortunately, my parents' dream of moving us to a gang-free environment was never realized—they were killed in a gang related drive-by shooting a week after my eleventh birthday.

 After their deaths, I was passed along from foster home to foster home. It took the government about two years to track down my only blood relative, an uncle that only lived about an hour away from me my entire life. There obviously must have been a good reason as to why my mother never wanted to reach out and contact her only living older brother and I later found out exactly what that reason was… and I found that information out the hard way.

 My Uncle Dennis Brown was the second person I have ever killed. I moved in with him and his wife Leslie when I turned thirteen. I was naïve and just happy to be out of foster care. It was so refreshing to be able to live with a blood relative again. At times I felt neglected in the foster homes I stayed in. I'd feel so unloved; some of my foster parents didn't even take the time to learn my name unless they were reading it on a check that the government had issued them for housing me. This is why the entire first year I moved in with my aunt and uncle I had never noticed any of Dennis' creepy gazes or remarks. For an entire year he showered me with love, attention, and a shoulder to cry on. Little did I know that every kind word or gesture administered to me by Dennis Brown was in exchange for my silence on the horrible things he would later do to me.

The nightmare began a little after my fourteenth birthday. I remember it like it was yesterday. Dennis came into my room late one night and woke me up while pulling up my night gown, ripping off my panties, spreading my legs, and then eating out my premature pussy.

"UNCLE DENNIS? WHAT ARE YOU DOING?" I shrieked once I was fully awake and aware of what was actually happening.

"SHUT UP GIRL BEFORE YOU WAKE UP YOUR AUNTY! —and I'm doing exactly what you want done to you! I know you're fourteen now and just started getting your period, which makes you a grown woman. Grown women have needs Jasmine… and I'm going to show you what those are." He said as he ignored my pleas and continued to eat my pussy.

"STOP UNCLE, PLEASE STOP!" I began to scream and cry, confused about what was occurring. Don't get me wrong. I knew everything about sex at the time. The Chicago school system didn't teach me what ocean bordered the west coast of the United States, but it definitely taught me that girls, *my age,* were having sex and getting pregnant. I was still a virgin thanks to the principles my parents had instilled in me since birth, but I was already crushing on boys from a distance, particularly a little fifteen-year-old popular boy named Edmond who lived down the street from me. Whenever Edmond and I rode bikes together I would imagine kissing him and more, so I wasn't completely innocent. Also I learned a lot from just listening to my peers and looking at the magazines and videos my uncle would recklessly leave around our home; sex wasn't at all new to me. However, what *was* new to me was that feeling of betrayal. My parents had loved me so unconditionally that I had no idea a blood relative of mine would've ever treated me worse than any foster family did. There I was almost falling in love with this man and revering him like my own father when BAM! In one instance he changed in my eyes completely. That night he not only ate my pussy, but he mounted me, held me down, beat me, and forced his enormous, adult sized, and unprotected penis inside of my vagina—stripping me of whatever innocence I had left.

When he finished inside of me he got up slowly and had zero signs of remorse in his eyes. The abuse had continued every night after that instance for months; he threatened to kill me if I ever told anyone. Afraid of being thrown out and given back to the government, I had no choice but to just internalize my pain. I had already developed abandonment issues by then, and despite the horrors I was facing in my uncle's care, the last thing I wanted was to go back into the system and have to start over and live with a completely different family. That would also mean I would possibly have to change schools and a new school would mean saying goodbye to the little bit of friends I had already made in this neighborhood… I just couldn't bear the thought of that—especially because that also meant saying goodbye to my biggest crush at the time; Edmond.

After some more months had passed my vagina began itching profusely to the point I finally couldn't keep the discomfort to myself. I ran to my aunt and told her something was devastatingly wrong with my privates, informing her in detail of all my discomfort. I told her about the smelly, yellow discharge and the fact that I had scratched myself so hard down there; it became tender and sometimes a little bloody. It ended up being a big mistake going to my aunt because she just ended up beating me that day. She whipped me with a belt until the skin on my back broke and bled, all the while calling me a "fast hoe". If only she knew the reason my vagina was in such terrible condition was because her evil husband had raped me every night for the past few months and had given me some sort of STD. So after everything was said and done, not only was I in dire pain because of the strange things occurring in between my legs, but also because of the sores my aunty dearest had left all across my back. I finally decided I couldn't keep my pain a family secret any longer. I was in way too much discomfort, and since trying to tell my aunt what I was going through didn't help me at all, the next school day I reported straight to the nurse's office.

"Jasmine, what's wrong?" Ms. Ellie, the kind nurse asked while attempting to console me.

"I can't stop itching down there." I cried in her arms as she wiped the tears that streamed down my face.

"Oh baby, you might just have a yeast infection, let me take you to a clinic after school." She insisted. Nurse Ellie went above and beyond for us students. She didn't have to help me; she could have sent me home with a note and passed the problem along to my family. After I expressed to her that I couldn't talk to my aunt and uncle about it, she took it upon herself to not only drive me to the nearby clinic after school, but she also waited with me there for hours, and paid the entire bill. That week is when I found out my uncle had given me chlamydia.

"Oh my God, Jasmine baby... who have you been sleeping with?" Nurse Ellie seemed shocked as we learned of the results together.

"A-a-boy." I lied, still afraid my uncle would make good on his promise and either kill me, or worse, abandon me. There was just no way in hell I was going to tell anyone that my own uncle had raped me and given me that STD. At the time I would rather have looked like 'a stupid teenage girl in love and having unprotected sex with a dirty teenage boy' than 'a helpless incest-rape victim'.

"Well you need to let that boy know *immediately* that he has given you an STD and that he needs to stop sleeping with you and any other girl until he gets himself treated." She lovingly advised me. "Do you hear me, Jasmine?"

"Yes Ms. Ellie." I responded.

"Good. I am so sorry you had to deal with these symptoms for weeks now because you were too embarrassed to tell your aunt and uncle." She said while hugging me. "Just take your medication for the time suggested and you should be all cleared up... and Jasmine, I know you're a growing girl and you have needs, but just make sure to use a condom whenever you have sex from now on. You're lucky that this time it was just chlamydia... next time it could be something more serious like a baby or God forbid—HIV." She was right but I cringed at the fact that she used the statement 'I had needs'. Those words triggered memories of the first night my uncle had raped me and the sick memories of that gruesome night flooded back into my head. I also trembled at the thought of catching something deadly like HIV from him. I remember thinking he probably did have HIV, after all he was an evil man and God always gave evil people what they deserved… right? After our long talk Nurse Ellie then gave me a twenty pack of condoms to take home with me, as well as the medication I had received from the clinic to cure my ailment.

I didn't get home until fairly late that day. I intentionally added a couple more hours to my walk home by repeatedly circling surrounding streets. I normally avoided aimless walking because my neighborhood was infested with drug dealers on almost every corner, but that day I needed the time alone. I was in deep thought trying to figure out how I was going to get my uncle to stop having sex with me, especially since I had just learned he had given me chlamydia.

"Where in the HELL have you been?" My drunken uncle stumbled out of the house screaming once he spotted me walking up on our stoop.

"I was at school talking to the nurse." I confessed somberly.

"The school nurse… WHY?" My uncle barked while reaching for and snatching the bag I had in my hand. "What the hell is this shit?" He continued while pulling out from the bag the medication and condoms I had received from the school nurse and the clinic.

"It's medicine… I have chlamydia." I truthfully disclosed.

"WHAT?" My uncle spat, his breath smelling like straight liquor.

"You gave me chlamydia!" I divulged right before bursting into tears. My uncle quickly grabbed the sides of my arms and squeezed with all his might.

"BITCH ARE YOU CRAZY? DON'T YOU EVER REPEAT THOSE WORDS AGAI--" Before he could even finish his sentence the neighborhood boy I had a crush on; Edmond, appeared out of nowhere on his bike.

"Hey Mr. Brown, can Jasmine come out and ride her bike with me?" My heart stopped. I had no idea how much Edmond had already seen or heard. I would have been absolutely horrified if my high school crush had ever found out that I had an STD. My uncle immediately loosened his grip from around my shoulders.

"No she's grounded." He informed Edmond.

"Grounded?" I wailed, "For what?" I would have wanted nothing more at that exact moment in my life than to have been able to ride my bike far, far away into the sunset. I would have loved to disappear with Edmond pedaling beside me escaping my uncle and this sorrow-filled life, but deep down I knew I was trapped.

"For being a fast little girl." Uncle Dennis snarled. "You see Edmond; Jasmine isn't the innocent fourteen-year-old girl you think she is. She's a fast little SLUT and she NEEDS to have her ass beat." He continued. I turned to look at Edmond who looked very angry at the moment. Obviously he believed my uncle and the year of innocent flirting we had built up was lost. Edmond was the reason I went to school, the reason I cared what my hair looked like, my only bit of happiness I had left in my life, and just like that my uncle had distorted Edmond's entire image of me. I could take the rape, the beatings, the threats, the verbal abuse, HELL… I was even about to let the chlamydia outbreak go… but the embarrassment he had caused me that night, outside on that stoop, in front of the then boy of my dreams, was the *last* straw and *extremely* unforgivable. On that day I made myself a mental note that that man was no longer my uncle, and in that very moment I vowed to destroy Dennis Brown. Being that I'm the type of person that brings objectives into fruition; Dennis' loose lipped betrayal would eventually cost him his life.

Chapter 4: The Love Child

~Present Day 2016~

"Congratulations, you're two months pregnant." I nearly faint at the words of my doctor.

"I'm what?" I ask in hopes of clarification.

"You're pregnant." My doctor reiterates (this time with less enthusiasm since my initial reaction was somewhat somber).

"How… how is this possible?" I ask a little more to myself than to Dr. Rinehart. Calvin Duggar can't have children; that is a known fact. Do you know how many groupies in the longevity of his music career attempted to pin babies on him, and time after time how many paternity tests have come back negative? Not to mention him and I have been having sex unprotected for the past ten years and this is the first time something like this has ever happened.

"Are you okay?" Dr. Rinehart inspects me while uncomfortably chuckling. His laughter snaps me out of my deep thinking.

"Yes. Yes, I'm fine. Thank you." I grab my jacket and run out of his office without waiting for further instruction. I asked the doctor earlier how this could possibly happen, but I knew damn well what the answer to that question was. It happened because two months ago I was having an affair with another man. Calvin couldn't and didn't knock me up—that other man did. I never thought I would ever have to deal with a juvenile situation like this again; I've only been pregnant once before and that was at an extremely young age… but here I am at thirty-seven, dealing with the same kind of bullshit.

I've cheated on Duggar before but two months ago was the first instance I not only cheated physically, but also emotionally. All the other times I've cheated I've always made sure to use protection, not only to prevent a pregnancy, but because I never wanted to experience catching an STD again. Going through all of that at the age of fourteen was reason enough for me to always stay protected, *except when it came to dealing with Calvin of course*. This new man has me all out of my element. Not only was I falling for him on a deeper level, but I had fucked him raw—and now I am pregnant with this love child… Oh what tangled webs we weave!

My first and only emotional affair is with a married man. The ordeal began as revenge sex. I hate his wife, and I thought what better way to get back at her than to fuck the shit out of her husband? —and I did. What I didn't plan on was acquiring deeply rooted feelings for him in the process, and now of course, actually getting pregnant.

As I drive home in complete silence I begin to think devilishly and concoct a plan. The man and I ended our affair almost as quickly as it began… well realistically, *he* ended it. Claiming he never actually wanted to cheat on his "perfect" wife and letting me know he was devastated and full of regret. Funny how men change as soon as they get what they want because I promise you before we actually 'did the do', he was all over me. Before anything even happened I asked him again and again if he was sure he could live with himself after we went all the way. He said yes, and he also told me in the heat of the moment that he loved me. Now he doesn't even return my phone calls and God forbid I spot him out in public he just walks fast in an opposite direction. I always used to wonder what his wife had that I didn't… and the answer to that just hit me this very moment. "I have a family" he would always say. "I can't just abandon my family", his words rang throughout my mind. *Well now he has a second family,* I think to myself as an enormous grin begins to appear on my face. Now I have some leverage over him. I finally have something his dearest wife had over me and it's currently growing inside of me. Initially I didn't know what I wanted to do about this pregnancy. For a split second I was considering aborting this innocent life, but now I'm realizing how much more valuable this baby is to me alive, and I suddenly want to keep it.

Of course I wouldn't abandon Duggar… He's my soul mate. We've been through and shared so much together and he needs me more than ever. I'm also pretty sure this new guy wouldn't just up and leave his wife and kids, but if I had this child… we would be forced to coexist, maybe even merge families. That's all I've ever really wanted; just to be a part of his life. He just keeps shutting me out, *STOP SHUTTING ME OUT DAMNIT!* I think to myself as tears stream down my face. My crying quickly turns into insane laughter as I pull into the driveway of my home. I am having this love child and there is nothing anyone can do about it. He will help raise and love our child… and eventually fall in love with me as well. Then I'll have both him and Duggar there by my side. How does that saying go again? —I want my cake and to eat it too!

When I unlock the door and walk inside my house I am hit by the stench of alcohol and some other disgusting odors. Duggar is pissy drunk and lying out on the living room sofa. I start to curse him out under my breath but decide not to wake him. Being the neat freak that I am, I immediately put down my bag and I start to clean up around him… that's when I find a woman's earring on the carpet underneath the couch—and it sure as hell isn't mine.

"YOU HAD THE AUDACITY TO BRING THAT HOE INSIDE MY DAMN HOUSE?" I scream at the top of my lungs which startles him out of his deep sleep.

"Yes man, damn." He jumps up. "I told your ass it was open season since you were out here doing you these past couple of months." He honestly admits. "What did the doctor say?" He asks giving me an evil eye.

"I'm two months pregnant." I speak solemnly.

"EXACTLY." Duggar laughs in a sad attempt to hide his pain. "And we both know that shit isn't even mine." He continues. At this moment my silence is worth a thousand words. "Yet your hypocritical ass is over here trippin' off of an earring and worrying about what I'm doing with my dick when you're in these streets being a flat out hoe!" I still don't say a word so he goes on with his rant. "I do me and you do you and that's how it's always been. So don't fucking ever come at me sideways again like we're some sort of fucking *Brady Bunch* or *Partridge Family*. You're just as fucked up as I am and it's even worse for you because now you have to go get that shit cut out of you!" He says pointing at my stomach. I know he's hurting, I would be equally as devastated if it was the other way around and he got one of his side hoes knocked up. Unfortunately, he crossed the line by bringing one of those desperate bitches inside my house, and I just wasn't going to let that slide.

"MOTHERFUCKER I DON'T GIVE A FUCK WHAT YOU DO WITH YOUR DICK JUST DON'T HAVE THAT BITCH MIYA, OR ANY OTHER FEMALE IN MY HOUSE AGAIN!" I say as I punch him in the arm and walk away, retreating to our bedroom. What Duggar doesn't know is that I wasn't going to abort this baby. It meant too much to me in the grand scheme of things. I just didn't want to break his heart tonight. Telling Duggar my plans of continuing this pregnancy would just be too much bad news to administer to him at once. I love Calvin and the last thing I ever want to do to him is destroy him emotionally.

    I fall backwards onto my bed with a big smile on my face. I can't believe I, Jasmine Hall, am going to be a mother. *I am going to be a great mother to you, just like my birth mother was to me, I promise you that.* I telepathically communicate to my unborn child. I begin to rub on my stomach for about an hour before eventually drifting into sleep.

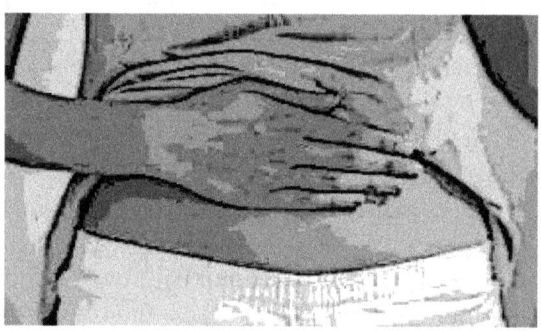

Chapter 5: Plan of Revenge

~Present Day 2016~

After I wake up, I'm still quite upset that Duggar had the nerve to bring another female into our home. We are both open cheaters, but I would never disrespect him to that extent. Sometimes I contemplate leaving Calvin for someone more respectful of my feelings; someone honest and loyal. Maybe Calvin brings out the worst in me and if I ever want to be a better person I need to be with someone that has a less similar background than my own. Jeremy Rogers would never disrespect his wife and have a side joint in their home. Who is Jeremy Rogers? Jeremy Rogers is not only the husband of my arch nemesis, Britney Greene (*now Britney Rogers*) ... but he is also my baby's father.

~Flashback 2006~

I met Jeremy Rogers the first and only time I ever attended the Annual Business Gala in DC. It was in 2006 when organizers of the ceremony honored Homeboy Duggar with a Lifetime Achievement of Excellence Award. Calvin Duggar is the only rap artist to have ever been esteemed with that honor. The year before the same award was given to Robert J. Aumann and Thomas C. Shelling for their work in Economics. Those two also won a Nobel Prize that same year for "having enhanced our understanding of conflict and cooperation through game-theory analysis". That goes to show how elite and prestigious it was to receive such an honor.

"Bullshit, they only gave it to me because I'm in a room full of people who I've signed shady contracts with throughout my career, and now that I'm a cripple, they want to toss my ass out like yesterday's news. You know they only gave me this honor thinking it would help me forgive them because they're not going to let me see a dime of my legacy until after I'm six feet deep." I remember a bitter Calvin growled into my ear the night of the gala... and he was right. It was really odd that he had been offered such a prominent award for just being a good rapper, even if he *was* one of the greatest rappers of our generation. That night he was even asked to perform a song of his choice; mind you, other than the orchestra that played underneath the main stage, in no prior ceremony had there ever been a musical act. Fittingly, Duggar chose to perform one of the first songs he'd ever released entitled "The Fakes All Around Me." Personally, it's one of my favorite songs of his.

    I grew up watching the Annual Business Gala on television. It is just as big as the Oscars and the Grammys except it lacks the entertainment portions and focuses on business excellence— (or as I like to put it the *real* money makers of every industry). In order for one to be invited to such a grandiose event, one would have to own or be associated with a business that raked in over eight million dollars that fiscal year. Of course a lot of musicians are always extended an invitation to the gala despite their income, *the same way some even attend white house correspondence dinners despite their knowledge of politics*, but to actually be HONORED at a gala placed Duggar on a completely different level than the rest. Whether or not this was to shut Duggar up and make him exit the industry quietly, while simultaneously handing over all the rights to his music to label executives was irrelevant—he would still be making history. After receiving a standing ovation for his performance (which Calvin executed entirely from a wheelchair) he somberly rolled back to our table and took his place next to me.

    The gala was beautifully decorated; I felt so out of place because everyone seated at our table was a millionaire except for me. I began to go down the table, read everyone's gold overlaid name plate, and google their net-worth from my cell phone. There were six other people at our table, Duggar of course was on my left and his name plate read: Calvin "Homeboy" Duggar – Platinum Recording Rap Artist/ Lifetime Achievement of Excellence Award Recipient 2006. I already knew Calvin's net-worth; it went from millionaire to FLAT BROKE after all the shady label deals fell through and the IRS swooped in to collect the rest of the money he owed in back taxes. To my right was an old gray haired man named Steven Ward. His name plate read: Steven G. Ward Jr. – American businessman, Philanthropist, Political Activist and chemical engineer. I didn't understand what any of that meant so I googled him and saw his net worth was close to forty BILLION dollars! Suddenly that old, overweight, grey haired man wasn't so bad on the eyes. I was honestly just happy to be in his presence. A lady with a name plate which simply read: Mrs. Ward sat to his right—that lucky bitch was set for life. Like me, she didn't have anything other than her name on her name plate. We were both there just riding the coat tails of our better halves. Seated next to Mrs. Ward was a scrawny, young, yet somewhat handsome looking man named Jeremy Rogers. What initially caught my attention was his curly jet black hair; it reminded me of my own uncontrollable mane of coils. He was also the only person—*other than Duggar and I*—who appeared to be under forty years old at our table. His gold plated nameplate read: Jeremy Rogers – Joint Owner of the TXA Radio Network. Once I googled him it wasn't his eighteen-million-dollar net-worth that stood out to me, it was the name under **spouse** that appeared on his Wikipedia that made me almost choke on my champagne. Right there in black and white it read [Spouse - Britney Rogers *(m. 2003- present)* formerly known as Britney Greene who is the Editor in Chief of the Tooley Times Newspaper]. *THAT BITCH!* I remember thinking when I came to the realization that the man who had been sitting across from me for the past hour and a half was the husband of my enemy.

    Britney Greene—now Britney Rogers—and I had history. That bitch did me so dirty years ago. Before I met Calvin, Britney was who I shared all my secrets with. I met her when I briefly worked for one of the most acclaimed law firms in North America; Hogan & Wildes, LLP. It was the year 2000 and we became instant friends. It only took a couple of months for me to begin loving her like the sister I never had. I looked up to that woman, she was five years older than me but her life looked so well put together. When I met her she was making over eighty thousand dollars a year, she was engaged and living in Tooley, she had a rags to riches story I was highly envious of, and she drove a Mercedes Benz. I came aboard at the firm as her subordinate. In the beginning everything went great, we got along so well, we both had horrible whore stories we shared with one another, but it all went downhill when she began to judge me and think she was better than me. The last time I spoke to Britney she hung up on me and told me she no longer wanted to be friends because she was moving on to bigger and better things and I would basically hold her back from greatness. It was at a time when I needed her most, I had just gotten fired and I really didn't want to go back to my old lifestyle of stripping. I defended that woman in some of her lower moments when we were co-workers, but she didn't give a single fuck about me. Out of everything I've been through and seen in my lifetime, Britney's behavior towards me really affected my self-esteem the most.

Anyways—so to my right, there sat her husband; Jeremy Rogers... and all I could honestly think about was how I was going to use this moment to initialize a plan of revenge. I still couldn't believe that she tossed our friendship aside because she didn't want to be associated with someone who led a lifestyle she was just as guilty of living—what a HYPOCRITE! I decided I was going to get her beloved husband Jeremy to fuck my brains out, record the whole ordeal on my cell phone, and then send the video to Britney. I cackled at the thought of her little heart breaking after she would not only discover her perfect husband's infidelity, but that he was cheating on her with ME of all people. Yea, I'm a cold bitch with abandonment issues, but I wanted her to feel the same emotional pain she had made me feel... then and only then would I be able to move on and let all this animosity I felt towards her go.

There are two parts to the Annual Business Gala; a serious more formal round table dinner and presentation, which takes place in an elegantly decorated, dimly lit auditorium and the second portion of the event is a more relaxed after party that takes place in a completely different (more ball-room-like-type) venue. This is where guests are supposed to let loose, have fun, drink, and dance. That night Duggar refused to go to the second portion of the occasion because he felt like he didn't have shit to celebrate in a room full of sharks. Initially I was going to be his 'ride or die' and stay in our hotel room with him all night, but I was way too tempted to execute my plan of fucking up Britney's life—so I ended up going to that party portion alone.

I waited until Duggar was fast asleep before I began to get dressed. The sedatives he took for the pain from his healing gunshot wound were extremely strong. (At the time his wound was fairly new and he had only been in a wheelchair for three months). He still to this very day has no idea that I ever even left his side that night. Wearing an extremely tight, nude, and skimpy latex dress, I stole some money and the after party passes from Duggar's coat pocket. I then caught a cab to the event alone.

I remember everyone at the after party being dressed like Cinderella and there I was wearing a twenty-dollar online boutique dress, but I swear I looked more appetizing than all of those millionaire housewives put together since no amount of money could ever buy a naturally jiggly ass like mine. Sure one could get injections or butt implants these days, but my ass is so real, round, and juicy—no plastic surgery could ever emulate my booty meat. When I walked into the venue all eyes were on me; I couldn't tell if people were looking at how cheap my dress was, how good my body looked, or deciding whether or not I actually belonged there since I wasn't accompanied by a known sponsor... regardless of it all they were still looking—and I thrived on the attention. I had one, and only one, purpose for being there that night and after a few drinks I began my hunt for revenge.

After hours of searching, I finally found Jeremy Rogers in the most humbling of places—chillin' behind the DJ booth. The DJ working the event looked somewhat star struck by Jeremy's presence. I bet he was in disbelief that this prominent radio executive even wanted to leave the company of rest of the millionaires in the room to mingle with little ole him. Despite Jeremy's financial and societal success, I guess he felt the DJ booth was still where he would feel the most comfortable. Wikipedia did mention he was a former DJ himself, so I assumed Mr. Rogers had a personal attachment and respect for those in the profession. Well he and I weren't so different in that aspect, don't get me wrong, I love money—but I'm a Chicago native at heart, and I was born and raised in the hood. I'd rather be amongst the poor and real, than the rich and fake.

"Jeremy?" I tapped on his shoulder after I approached the DJ booth.

"Yes?" Jeremy turned around looking a little shocked that I even knew his name. That's when I think he recognized me from the table at the first half of the gala. "Oh hey, you're the young lady that sat near me right... Homeboy Duggar's date?"

"Yea that's me." I chuckled. "I'm his family member." I lied. The purpose of the interaction was to get the man to sleep with me; he was already married so it wouldn't make sense to give him another reason to have doubts about sleeping with me. Selling myself as a single woman would give me a better chance with a good-boy-geek like him.

"Oh okay, what's your name?" He politely asked while shaking my hand and handing me one of his business cards.

"Ivy." I lied again. *Poison Ivy to you and your wife,* I thought.

"Nice to meet you, Ivy." He spoke hinting at wanting to conclude our conversation. Paparazzi were swarming the place, and I'm sure the last thing Jeremy wanted was to be pictured in a tabloid, standing next to a woman in a skimpy latex dress. It just wouldn't look right, especially since we were way off in a secluded corner by the DJ booth. These galas were notorious for being the root of a lot of celebrity sex scandals, whether they ended up being true or not—Even Britney experienced falling victim to the tabloids after attending her first Annual Business Gala, *with our then boss,* in the year 2000.

"Yea it was. Hey can I ask you a question? I don't really know where to book a room tonight. You see Duggar and I are sharing a room and he has a lot of groupies over right now and I'm not trying to hear a family member indulge in orgies all night. I asked our establishment for a separate room but they're completely booked. Could you recommend a hotel establishment, maybe the one you're currently staying in?" I asked with a hidden agenda. Once I discovered what hotel Jeremy was staying in, I planned on actually meeting him in his room.

"Really? Even though he's in a wheelchair—never mind don't answer that—um I'm staying at the Ritz-Carlton Hotel in Northwest, I highly recommend it… I believe it's on 22nd street. I honestly think you're going to be out of luck though, because it might be completely booked as well. People book hotel rooms for this event months in advance. I doubt there are any rooms left *anywhere* in DC. You might want to go look further away from the city… try southern Maryland or Virginia." He informed me.

"Okay thanks." I responded walking away, pretending our communication was over. Little did he know him and I had MUCH MORE business to take care of.

I left the after party immediately, hours before it was due to end, after Jeremy had given me the information I needed. I hailed another cab, this time to the Ritz-Carlton. I sat in the busy lobby for about thirty minutes 'casing the joint'. It was really crowded for it to be so late at night; I'm guessing with all the events that were taking place in DC surrounding the gala, every location would remain this busy into the morning. Once I figured out who was who and where every Ritz-Carlton employee was, I made my move. I scurried to the women's restroom that was located in the lobby and quickly created a big mess. I rubbed the lipstick that was in my purse all over the mirrors, at times spelling out obscenities. I used paper towels to clog up all the sink holes, turned on their faucets and let the water run; each sink eventually overflowed and leaked onto the floor. I also grabbed a ton of toilet paper and just teepeed the entire vicinity. In less than ten minutes I was able to turn that immaculate facility into a pigsty with surprisingly no interruption. Then calmly, and before anyone else entered, I stormed out of the women's bathroom and stomped straight up to the front desk.

"Excuse me, but I am disgusted at the condition of your restroom. I am waiting on a friend of mine who's booked a room here tonight and I might just have to advise him to check out immediately." I barked at the front desk clerk.

"Oh dear, I'm terribly apologetic about your experience ma'am. I could have sworn housekeeping *just* finished cleaning the restrooms down here in the lobby less than thirty minutes ago. I guess with the traffic we're encountering this weekend our staff should be more vigilant." He then immediately picked up the phone. "Yes, Amy? Could you please come down here right this minute and check the lobby restrooms? ...Yes... I know you've just cleaned it... exactly... Thank you. *click*—again ma'am I am so sorry you had to deal with that." He continued.

"It's fine. I'll go wait by the door for housekeeping. It was so messy I didn't even get a chance to use it!" I continued. Embarrassed, the nervous clerk simply nodded. I stood by the restroom door and in less than two minutes a maid in uniform scurried past me and went into the bathroom pushing a mop bucket and cleaning supplies. She barely even noticed me standing there; poor thing was so focused on keeping her job she got straight to work. She didn't even notice I had snuck in behind her and locked the bathroom door from the inside.

That's when the-old-me took over in the moment and I grabbed a hold of a bottle from her cleaning supplies and knocked the frail young woman over her head. She fell to the ground immediately. The maid couldn't have weighed more than a hundred pounds total. I grabbed tissue from a stall and masking tape from her provisions, and confined her. I then undressed the woman and switched clothes with her. She murmured for help but there was no use, I tapped her mouth shut and her hands were tied behind her back. She was also still very weak from the blow to her head so she barely put up a fight. I learned how to knock people out and then rob them from my early Chi-town days, so I was able to put my former training in use. I hid the defeated maid on the floor in the handicapped stall.

"I'm sorry." I whispered to her once the coast was clear and I locked the stall she was in from the inside then crawled underneath it to escape. I also went to the mirror to adjust my make-up and the uniform. The skirt portion of the outfit barely fit around my ass but I made it work. I knew exactly what to do and I maintained my composure even when I heard hotel guests impatiently pulling on the locked restroom door. When I finally left the bathroom I locked it with one of the master keys I had found in the maid's possession, this was to prevent anyone else from being able to enter. I knew I had a good couple of hours to execute my plan before being discovered. Not only did I take the maid's keys and mop bucket, I also took her Walkie-Talkie. I listened in on the other hotel staff on the line and observed how they communicated.

"This is Amy" I tried my best to imitate the maid's voice that I had just hijacked, "I'm going to be in the women's bathroom in the lobby for a while, some kids or drunks must have been in here because it's a complete mess. If you need me hit me on my Walkie… also does anyone know what room our guest Jeremy Rogers is staying in? He told me he was out of towels this afternoon; I want to go take care of that before he gets in."

"Copy that, Amy. Rogers is in room 523." An unknown voice responded. *That was almost too easy,* I thought to myself. Taking the emergency staircase to avoid contact and suspicion from other hotel employees, I made my way to the fifth floor dressed like a maid. When I arrived at room 523 I took out a key that read *fifth floor master* and I tried it on Jeremy's door. Like magic it worked instantly. I remember being in disbelief at how smoothly my plan was being executed. As soon as I stepped foot in the room I began doing a victory dance, I couldn't believe I was now inside Jeremy Rogers' suite. The first thing I did was go to the balcony and toss out the two-way radio. I had no idea whether or not the hotel establishment had installed a tracking device in it and I wanted to avoid discovery at all cost. I then immediately began to strip out of the maid uniform.

Once I was finished getting rid of all the incriminating evidence, I completely undressed, and after making sure the door was double locked I immediately hopped in the shower. I washed my entire body thoroughly especially my cooch and got ready for what I expected would be a great night. There is NOTHING sexier than ill-intentioned, resentful, and *illegal* sex—and I had definitely broken at least one kidnapping law to get there. After my shower I oiled my body from my head to my toe with some expensive oils I found in Jeremy's gift basket… I then laid entirely naked in his bed.

Finally, after some hours had passed, I heard Jeremy arrive. When he opened the door to the room and saw me on his bed I could tell he had been startled close to death because he immediately jumped back losing his balance.

"WHAT THE HELL IS THIS?" He shrieked. "Ivy? What are you doing here? How'd you even get in here? —you almost gave me a heart attack!"

"Calm down baby." I got up slowly and seductively and strutted naked towards him, closing the door behind him. "Come sit down on the bed with me." I smirked. We were both a little tipsy, him from the gala, and me from helping myself to his minibar. A lot of alcohol is always served at the gala so Jeremy was just as lit as I was. We both had red blood shot eyes, from both fatigue and inebriation.

"I can't—I can't do this." He shook his head trying not to stare at my beautiful succulent body.

"It's all yours, daddy, I know you want it." I breathe onto his neck, pulling him closer to my body and the bed. Jeremy starkly pushed me off him and continued to make his way towards the door.

"Put your clothes on girl, I'm calling security, THIS IS CRAZY!" He said adamantly.

"Why baby?" I asked, a little sad that he wasn't even giving me a chance to explain anything. I had to try harder; I hopped on the bed and spread my legs in his direction, exposing my pretty, shaved, pink pussy. I then began to finger myself and rub my clit grandiosely. "Please fuck me daddy."

"Ivy I'm happily married… YOU REALLY NEED TO LEAVE. You know what, never mind. I'LL GO." At that point he was exasperated. I was a little scared he would go straight to security or the front desk so I wasn't going to just let him walk out while I was lying there naked.

"Oh really? You're just going to leave me?" I barked trying to stall for time.

"Damn right." He reiterated.

"Fine." I gave up and began to pick up pieces of the maid's garb that were spread out across the floor. "I don't have any clothes that actually fit, can I borrow some of yours and then I'll be out of your life forever I promise."

"Yea, whatever." He rolls his eyes, "Just cover up!"

"Go ahead and pretend you don't want my pussy when we both know you do, but don't pretend you're in an amazing relationship when we both know you're married to the devil." I slurred.

"What are you even talking about?" Jeremy bellowed frustrated.

"She's cheated on you over and over again in the past!" I reminded him.

"That was before we got married, and how do you even know about that—WHO THE HELL ARE YOU? Is this a test?" He asked frustrated.

"NO! I'm just a former friend of hers. Look, I know what the fuck she's put you through because she's told me. I even know stuff she probably has never even confessed to you. Here's my number…" I grabbed a hotel pen from the dresser and wrote my number inside the palm of his hand. "That's so you can call me when you get home, back to Missouri. We can exchange war stories then. I know for a fact she's just like me—devilish. And if she's your type, I must be too." I laugh as I leave his room in his dress shirt and slacks.

That night I miraculously managed to escape the establishment without being caught. I walked right passed all the police in the lobby who were surrounding Amy, the crying maid. I giggled at the thought of how she even managed to escape. Even though my mission was a fail after meeting Jeremy, I was still happy I managed to avoid catching a case in DC—I hear their jails are unbearable.

After that initial encounter days turned to months, and months turned to years, but he never called. He wasn't even curious about me, which is what made ME even more curious about him. What started out as me chasing him for revenge sex turned into me being genuinely interested in the type of loyal person he was. I was naked and available and he turned me down. I had never before in my lifetime come across a good, faithful guy like him. He reminded me of how loyal my father was to my mother. I was extremely jealous of what Britney had after that day. What made her deserve that kind of love?

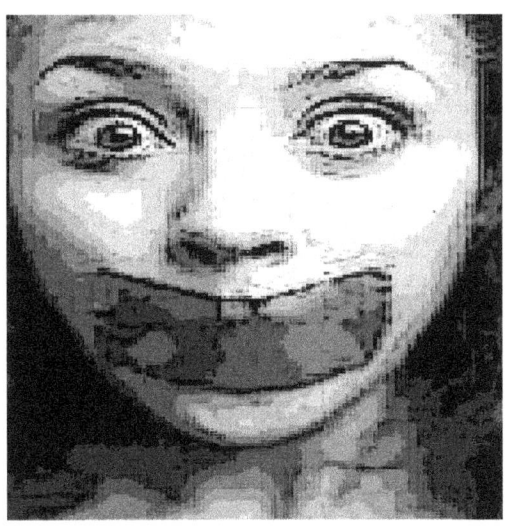

Chapter 6: Blank Tombstones

~1992-1996 Flashback~
  Dysfunctional relationships are nothing new to me. In fact, *aside from my Uncle Dennis*, Gary "Killa" Lewis was my first lover. I remember seeing him for the first time when I was thirteen and had only been living with my uncle and aunt for two months. Killa had to be sixteen at the time; he was always posted up at the same street corner directly adjacent to my uncle's house. I was so dumb and naïve at the time but of course now I know that back then, the reason he was on street corners was because he was selling drugs. I thought he was cute back then, but there was always something cold about him that I wanted nothing to do with. It sometimes felt like he was a soulless boy when I'd see how he treated all the other kids in my neighborhood, especially my then crush; Edmond. He stole bikes, bullied, and beat up innocent children for their shoes and money, most of the time showing absolutely no mercy. I remember one day I witnessed him bludgeoning a man twice his age to a bloody pulp, so regardless of how handsome I thought he was *(even at age thirteen)* I was wise enough to stay clear of that devil.
  The older I became, the less I saw of Killa in my neighborhood, however that did nothing to slow down the fear that was associated with his name in the streets. He had moved up in the ranks of the drug game and was replaced on the block with another much frailer boy. Killa was definitely out of sight but not out of mind; he would show up from time to time in the neighborhood and be completely unforgiving when owed a debt. Even my uncle learned that the hard way, you see Dennis used to buy his drugs from Killa but began to do business with the new weaker kid, *whose name I never learned*. I had to be about fifteen when I came home from school one day and the boy was pleading with my uncle to pay up what he owed him from a previous drug sale.
  "P-p-please Dennis, I like you, don't make me have to involve Killa." The boy stuttered. Poor thing had to be no older than fourteen, and although I'm sure he had a gun on him, he had the aura of a coward. I remember Killa was the complete opposite with unsympathetic fearless eyes; my uncle would have never tried that shit with him. This new kid lacked that authoritative nature so

naturally my cowardly uncle took advantage of that weakness. I swear that man had a thing for preying on the feeble at heart.

"I don't give two shits who you involve, I already payed you." My uncle chuckled at the desperate boy who was close to tears. Anyways, weeks passed after that incident and that frail kid immediately went missing. Some say Killa gunned him down for not being able to control his customers. Can you imagine getting killed for not killing when you were owed money? —shit was unreal! I remember one day soon after, I was walking home from school when I saw three cars speed into my uncle's driveway and the passengers in those vehicles began letting off rounds in the air.

"WHAT THE HELL?" I screamed as I ducked in my neighbors bushes for safety. Just then I saw none other than Killa exiting from the back of one of the cars. The last time I saw the teen he was young and unfriendly… but this older, eighteen-year-old adult-version of Killa looked a little less scary and a lot more debonair and successful. He made his way to our front door, adjusted his suit jacket and politely knocked as if he wasn't a part of the speeding car spectacle that had just occurred. I was close enough to hear and see everything that was happening but well-hidden enough to stay safe and unseen. I saw my aunt slowly open up the front door, she was trembling uncontrollably.

"Leslie, is Dennis home?" A calm and collected Killa asked my unsteady aunt.

"No… no… he's not in right now." *Oh hell nah*! I thought to myself after she lied through her teeth for my treacherous uncle. That man is so lowly he sent his wife into harm's way to answer the door and lie on his behalf. I swear at the time he was probably nestled underneath their mattress. I knew damn well Dennis was home at that exact moment, he was just hiding because he knew he owed Killa some serious drug money. My aunt loved and would blindly defend my uncle to her last breath, she was always turning a blind eye to his despicable ways—but I wasn't my aunt, and this whole ordeal had been very entertaining for me up until that point. How dare my Aunt Leslie attempt to stop the sidesplitting comedy show that was unfolding? So naturally, being the rebellious teen that I was, I got up from those bushes QUICK and scurried to my aunt's side.

"I'm pretty sure Uncle Dennis is home." I correct my aunt in front of Killa who, mind you, was even sexier up close and personal. Couldn't take my eyes off of him, I fell in love with him as he stood there putting the fear of God into my tormenters—*I mean*—guardians.

"Shut up, girl!" My aunt spat; attempting to hush me. If looks could kill I would have been dead that very moment, because she followed that command with a look of death. The way I saw things back then, whether or not I kept my mouth shut in that moment I would still be getting a beating, which is why I decided to not 'shut up' and egg the situation on. Plus, my 'big and bad' uncle had been exerting his authority over me almost every night for the past year and a half so I remember thinking it would be sweet justice to see Killa give him a taste of his own medicine.

"Jasmine?" Killa interrupted the moment and looked me over while chuckling. "Little Jasmine?"

"What's up, Killa?" I blushed. I knew what he was shocked by; that the thirteen-year-old girl he used to know who rode her bike up and down the block was gone. The little stick figure that he once paid no attention to had grown into a lovely *plump* and delectable flower. I was still a good girl at heart and had never given myself willingly to a man, but my body definitely spoke otherwise. My hips and lips were full grown and voluptuous.

"Yo, you're looking good little lady, looking *really* good. You're still a good little school girl right?" He joked flirtatiously.

"Of course." I smiled.

"Can you guys take this somewhere else?" My aunt snapped forgetting she was snapping at a killer. She always got jealous when any man would give me attention, whether it was her husband or the mail man. She was livid that my body was growing into its own. I naturally took after my curvy, yet in shape mother… My Aunt Leslie however had the shape of a vending machine and got zero attention for it.

"Don't you see us talking?" Killa snapped right back at my aunt making her stumble backwards a little bit. Killa then took out a piece of paper and scribbled his phone number on it. "Since you're the only one here with any sense, Jasmine, when you see your PUNK ASS uncle, tell him he'd better get my money ready, because the next time me and my goons show up it's not going to be a friendly visit." He barked more towards my aunt as he handed me the paper. Then he turned and walked down the stoop and got back into his car. Killa and his goons immediately sped out the driveway and left with my heart.

After that ordeal, I used that number to contact Killa on my own and a steamy relationship between him and I blossomed and became intense within a matter of months. Of course my uncle ended up paying him back every dime of his money (with interest), but after he noticed Killa and I became an item he began to fear me as well. Uncle Dennis never touched me again after Killa and I went on our first date. If Killa was willing to catch a case for the three hundred dollars my uncle owed him, imagine what he'd do if he found out my uncle was pushing up against his girl. I was Killa's first public girlfriend EVER, and every female in my neighborhood was jealous of our union. I was the first girl he would buy clothes and shoes for; I mean he took extraordinarily good care of me. I ended up moving out of my uncle and aunts house and living in Killa's big house about an hour away. I bonded with Killa and his army of goons; they became like family to me and respected me as Killa's queen. We all lived in that house together and even though a lot of fucked up shit occurred under that roof, I didn't contest it because it felt like home.

I became a very bad girl myself by association. Killa and his gang brought out the tiger in me. I was equally as heartless and cold. They taught me that the world is a cold ass place, either hunt or be hunted. Life became all about money and power. When I turned sixteen we developed a system that expanded how the squad acquired income. The other girlfriends of gang members living in the house and I were given fake IDs and sent out to 'hunt'. Killa would tell us to go to clubs all over Chicago and pick up rich sucker drug dealers. [A rich sucker drug dealer or a mark was a guy (most likely from out of town), who would come to Chicago clubs in Lamborghini's showing off, wearing about six or seven chains around their necks. We knew they had mad money, but we could also see the green, naïve side to them. Plus, none of them would ever dare go to the police because they had rap sheets themselves, which made them easy ass targets]. "Those types of lames deserve to be robbed", Killa would often justify, "How dare they come to OUR fucking city and flaunt their fucking wealth so disrespectfully?"

He told me to sell myself as a prostitute and convince the 'rich suckers' that for a fee, they could meet up with me at a hotel and have all their wishes granted. Killa knew I was one of the best looking girls in the crew so I was always booking these rich marks. The men would promise me hundreds of dollars for a taste of my young ass, the only catch was I never had to actually sleep with any of them. Killa and his men would always bust down the door in the nick of time and rob the marks for everything they had with them (car, watch, phone, money, wallet, credit cards, clothes, shoes, chains, ear rings, etc.…) My only job was to get them alone, make sure they were actually from out of town, make sure they were actually rich, and never let any of them touch me. Killa stressed the last point tremendously, "DO NOT LET THEM MOTHERFUCKERS PUT A HAND ON YOU!" He would growl. Once the robbery occurred, us girls were to pretend we were just as shocked as the marks and act as though we were getting robbed our damn selves. We had perfected the routine and were coming out of each situation with thousands of dollars in profit a night.

As sick as our relationship seemed, I could tell Killa loved and adored me. I remember one-night communication was off and one of the rich suckers I had in a hotel room had managed to pounce on me and attempted to rape me before I could even get a signal to Killa.

"STOP!" I screamed! "Please stop!" And in that moment I began having intense flashbacks of the horror my uncle put me through.

"Nah bitch, you think I would actually pay for pussy? You have me fucked up! I'm 'bout to take this shit and throw you out of my damn room." The mark snarled. By the time Killa and his boys eventually busted down the door the man had already gotten as far as ripping off my dress. Killa got extremely belligerent and out of character when he saw what was happening—at least way angrier than usual.

"ARE YOU TRYING TO GET FRESH WITH MY BITCH?" He roared at the extremely startled man who began to pee on himself. I scurried off the bed and ran to a secluded corner of the room where I stood in my bra and underwear.

The thing I loved about Killa was he changed every instance of my life where I've been victimized into a triumph. Just minutes earlier I was cowering, but now I was screaming obscenities at the pleading man with the rest of my very big crew. In that moment I knew I was forever safe and if any man ever tried to disrespect me Killa would kill them before they had a chance to. I had always heard rumors of how Killa acquired his nickname but that night was the first time I saw his rage first hand. After waving his gun madly, Killa then placed the barrel of it right on the temple of the whimpering mark and without remorse, began pulling the trigger. POW! POW! POW! POW! POW! Five shots to the head… then that was it, the man was obliterated, face damaged beyond recognition.

I stood there mesmerized, not at all frightened by what had just occurred, I just remember absorbing in the moment. I saw power in death, Killa's actions were infinite, and he possessed the strength and fearlessness to end lives; after that he became like a god to me. I had never felt freer from worry in my entire life. "NO MAN IS TO EVER LAY A HAND ON MY WOMAN!" Killa howled to no one in particular as he stayed in place and spit on the man's corps. His prepared goons got into action placing the body in a bag and cleaning up the crime scene.

"Come on baby!" Killa yelled to me after we caught wind of the police sirens in the distant night. Everyone knew that was our cue to get the hell away from the hotel establishment. I grabbed my clothes while Killa pocketed the mark's diamond encrusted watch and wallet (which had about four thousand dollars in it) and we all began running like the wind. His crew members with the body in their trunk sped off in one direction while Killa and I headed home in his car. He was the Clyde to my Bonnie… we were truly a sick and demented match made in heaven.

That night we celebrated evading capture and Killa and I got really drunk and high and laid up in his bed just talking about life. I assumed that the rest of his goons were still out getting rid of the body and evading police because the house was so quiet you could hear a pin drop. We weren't worried about the owners of the hotel talking or any witnesses because they were in fear of their lives and knew there would be repercussions from Killa's camp. Getting away with murder gave me a thrill I would never be able to match for the rest of my life.

"I love you; you see how I just killed for you at the drop of a dime right?" He said slurring his words. "I fucking love you, you're my fucking woman. No one is allowed to touch you but me, NO ONE." He ranted.

"I'm all yours baby." I responded back equally as faded. "I love you too my king, my hero!" We began to kiss and make continuous love. Killa was really introverted. I mean, we would stick up those rich naïve drug dealers together, we would shop together, we lived together, but our relationship was still pretty shallow… until that night. That's the night Killa told me his real name for the first time in our year long relationship. He even opened up about his child hood, and all the sick shit he'd done in the past.

"Thoman Fendy." I remember him randomly saying hours later.

"Who?" I asked in confusion, my eyes still closed as I had been asleep on his chest.

"The guy's name we shot earlier; it's Thoman Fendy." He reiterated.

"Okay?" I asked still lost as to why he was bringing that up. Opening my eyes, I saw he had the man's wallet in his hand.

"You never realized I had tattoos of the names of all the people whose lives I've taken?" He asked somberly referring to all his ink.

"No… I just thought those were family members or something." I responded honestly. Getting up from Killa's chest I turned him onto his stomach so I could get a better view of the art that ran across his entire back. I had never really paid attention to any of it until the moment he had said something; not to mention Killa was already very dark skinned with a beautifully flawless complexion, so his tattoos weren't all that visible to begin with. I began to run my fingertips delicately over the raised tattoos that covered his torso and realized I was looking at hundreds of tiny tombstones, most with names in them… but a few empty ones.

"Oh my God baby, you killed all these people?" I gasped in excitement. I remember thinking if it was true he definitely earned his nickname. Years earlier, before my uncle ever laid in my bed, if I had known this about Killa it would have immediately turn me off, but at that stage in my life I was so emotionally numb from the abuse I endured that, I actually was slightly turned on by this revelation.

"You still love me don't you?" He begged me for reassurance.

"Of course baby, we're Bonnie and Clyde, I'll be your ride or die." I reassured him meaning every word I spoke. We started to kiss passionately. "But what are those blank tombstones for?" I couldn't help but probe.

"Killing comes with the territory of being a god, Jasmine. Even the God in heaven gives life and takes it away. My daddy was a killer, my uncle was a killer, and their daddy was a killer before them. I already know what I inherited, what I was destined for. Those tombstones are for the lives I have yet to take. It's a kill or be killed world out in these Chicago streets baby, and I don't plan on becoming prey anytime soon." He coldly informed me. His words solidified my complete loyalty, trust and love for Gary "Killa" Lewis. He was my god, my provider, and my protector. I was ready to get on my knees and worship him. He gave me a great life, and loved me so passionately I no longer mourned my parents. He taught me that with life comes death, making death inevitable; this notion made me begin to appreciate life even more—but in the same instance, I no longer feared death. Since Killa had opened up about his past and had enlightened me, I figured I'd do the same thing in that moment and just completely be honest with him about my own family secrets.

"Since we're being honest and all, I have a confession." I let out meekly.

"What is it baby?" He purred while playing in my curly hair. I was lying naked snuggled close to his beautiful body, smoking a joint.

"Well…" I exhaled the marijuana smoke before passing the weed to him. "Remember when we first started messing with each other and you asked me was I a virgin?" Before I could even finish my confession, Killa violently jumped off the bed pushing me off of him.

"YOU JUST LIKE THE REST OF THESE BITCHES AREN'T YOU?" He screamed out of nowhere at the top of his lungs. "I WASN'T YOUR FIRST WAS I?" He barked even louder.

"Baby… calm down…" I tried to let out before I felt his hand come down with all its might, slapping me on the side of my face. I was in shock so I just froze up and sat there; tasting the blood from my busted lip… he had NEVER before EVER laid a hand on me.

"YOU ARE JUST LIKE THEM OTHER BITCHES! SAME SHIT KILLED MY FATHER! DIRTY BITCHES LIKE YOU GAVE HIM AIDS!" He screamed at the top of his lungs. It was almost as though a demon had taken over his body, even his pupils became dilated. He began dragging me across the room by my hair.

"Baby, please!" I let out in between sobs. "I didn't sleep with anyone else; I was raped by a family membe--" SMACK! Before I could even finish my sentence he struck me again, this hit more painful than the first. The blows became continuous and went on for what felt like an eternity, blow after blow to my body and face. I didn't understand what was so wrong about my confession then, but years later when I really reflected on the moment I came to the conclusion the reason he was so pressed about whether or not I was a virgin when we first met was because he had a fear of contracting HIV. Gary "Killa" Lewis, the only man I ever knew who wasn't afraid of ANTHING including death itself was afraid of going out the same way his father did—AIDS. I had no idea whether I was the first girl he ever made love to, or if Gary only had sex with virgins… or maybe the reason he revered me was because I was the first virgin he ever dealt with… whatever his reasoning, had I been a virgin initially THAT ENTIRE EPISODE WOULD HAVE NEVER HAPPENED— so naturally in that moment, I blamed my uncle for ruining me.

After Killa beat me to a pulp and made me sleep on the floor, he downed a whole fifth of Hennessey and passed out for the night. That's when I was left alone in my head, and because I hadn't been with any other man I assumed this is how my life would play out forever. I truly believed that if I ever opened up and became completely honest with ANY man about my incestualized past, they would beat me. I was angrier that my uncle had ever molested me in the first place than I was about Killa putting his hands on me. So that night I decided on the spot to kill my uncle for giving me this mark of shame (even though at the time I hadn't even seen him in over a year). What he did to me not only affected me mentally and physically for the rest of my life, but now relationship-wise as well? HELL NO! I was done being a slave to his transgressions.

    Around four in the morning, while it was still pitch black outside, I went to Killa's hiding place and retrieved the gun he used earlier to kill the man in the hotel room. I loaded it up with more bullets, took Killa's car keys out of his back pocket, wore one of his black hoodies, snuck out of his house, and drove to my uncle's house in the projects about an hour down the road. I parked outside of the house I used to call home drinking heavily for a couple of minutes before I decided to eventually exit the car. I quietly snuck through the back door, which I already knew they kept unlocked due to living with them for three years. I cocked the gun while I was still downstairs so that all I would need to do once in their bedroom was aim and shoot at my uncle. When I reached the top of the staircase my heart began to pound profusely. What was I doing? —was I really about to kill a man? Then I began having flashbacks of all the nights I was tortured under that very roof and all the reconsideration left my body immediately. I quickly busted into my aunt and uncle's room, aimed at my uncle's temple and with no remorse, pulled the trigger—it was finished. I remember his brains splattered all over the walls due to the fact I had fired from close range. Before my Aunt Leslie even sat up and realized what was happening her husband was dead and I had already raced down the steps, through the back door, and hoped into Killa's car, speeding off into the night.

    When I got back to Killa's house I was shaking. I quietly closed the door, put his car keys back into his pocket, placed the gun back in its hiding place and removed the hoodie and gloves, throwing them in the laundry room. I then curled back into a ball on the floor; my adrenaline pumping, feeling a sick sense of nirvana. Not even fifteen minutes had passed of me positioning myself on the floor before I heard a loud BOOM coming from the front door, sirens, and helicopters surrounded the house.

    FUCK! I thought to myself, *how the fuck did they find me?* I began to wake Killa's drunken ass up. "WAKE THE HELL UP! THE POLICE ARE HERE! I DID SOMETHING STUPID BABY!" I cried out.

"WHAT? HUH?" He said confused and still a bit tipsy from all the alcohol he consumed. I gave up trying to explain shit to his plastered ass and ended up just curling up in a ball, mentally preparing myself to surrender.

"COME OUT WITH YOUR HANDS UP, WE HAVE YOU SURROUNDED!" I hear a police officer yell from outside our bedroom.

"Fuck that, I'm going out blazing!" Killa—finally alert—said with every intention of getting up and retrieving his gun. He had always told me he would rather die than willfully submit to police custody, and I believed him, unfortunately for him before he could even get to the gun, policemen busted down the bedroom door and aimed their guns at both of us.

"SURRENDER GARY, IT'S TOO LATE FOR YOU NOW, WE HAVE YOUR ENTIRE HOUSE SURROUNDED!" I heard an officer say. That's when I realized—wait a minute; these officers weren't there to arrest me! They were there to take down Killa, and after they forcefully apprehended him a detective came and pulled me aside.

"Are you okay?" I remember the detective asking me in a heartening way referring to my beaten face, I nodded. "Is your name Jasmine?" He continued his inquiry; I could sense genuine concern coming from his body language.

"Yes—yes it is." I stuttered. "What's happening?"

"Well your Aunt made a call to us over an hour ago. She claimed Gary, the man you know as Killa, just left her house and shot and killed your uncle in his sleep." Wait, wait, wait, I thought to myself while doing a mental victory lap in my head. Not only did I kill my uncle *who was the devil reincarnated*, but I now had a chance to pin the whole ordeal on the man who just beat me to a pulp hours earlier? This was karma at its finest. I felt empowered in that very moment and thought to myself; such would be the fate of any man in my life from here on out that ever mistreated me—death or incarceration.

"OH MY GOODNESS! HE KILLED MY UNCLE?" I gave an extravagant performance and fell to the ground "MY DEAR UNCLE OH MY GOD, THAT MONSTER!" I cried.

"Jasmine, what the fuck?" I could hear Gary yelling at me from the other room where he was being held captive by three heavily armed officers. "TELL THEM I WAS HERE ASLEEP WITH YOU ALL NIGHT!" He yelled to me.

That's when I motioned to the officer directly in front of me to lean in closer to me because I was frightened. "He was gone all night and he told me he was going to do this. My uncle owed him drug money a while back. He's been holding me hostage for the past year. He got extremely drunk and started beating on me for no reason. Then he drank an entire bottle of Henny, that's when he stormed out of the house and I had no idea where he was going. He literally just got back in fifteen minutes before you guys arrived."

"I've heard enough. Guys read him his rights and take him down town!" He yelled to the officers who were with Killa. "I can't believe we finally got him! Young lady you are a hero, we have been waiting years to take this filthy man off the streets but everyone was too scared to point him out and we could never find any dirt on him. You are a hero. I am deeply sorry about your uncle." That's when I heard them finally reading Killa his rights and saw them carry him outside to their police car.

"YOU BITCH; I'M GOING TO FUCKING KILL YOU! YOU SET ME UP! YOU BITCH!" He growled from outside. I'm not even going to lie, as empowered as I felt; those were chilling words to hear. I had no doubt in my mind that if Gary ever escaped prison or got loose that he would come back and kill me, I even feared one of his goons coming after me that same night. A little freaked out about repercussions I made sure to give the officers a lot more incriminating evidence that would put him and his entire gang away for the rest of their lives.

While downtown being interviewed I told the police where they could find the gun, I told them about the Thoman Fendy murder that occurred the night before and I told them the meanings of all the tattoos across his back. I also told them the ins and outs of the drug organization Killa ran. Not only was my account enough to put him away for life, but my aunt's testimony also backed up what I said to a T. She recognized his hoody and car and further identified him as the killer, so did a lot of neighbors and witnesses from her house back to Killa's neighborhood. No one thought it was me driving that car so recklessly; no one suspected it was little ole me who pulled the trigger. The police even sympathized with me and released my under-aged ass to my aunt's custody. They referred to me as a hero for putting the murderous, nineteen-year-old Gary "Killa" Lewis and friends away for good—and I accepted all the praise, sympathy, and accolades without any remorse.

"AUNTY!" I ran to her sobbing once we were finally allowed to see each other.

"Yes baby, I'm here." She was visibly a wreck following the death of her husband. I couldn't believe, one, that she believed my bullshit ass story about not being involved in my uncle's death at all, and two, that I had been kidnapped by Killa this entire time. She consoled me saying "We're going to get through this; I know you loved Dennis too baby, we're going to get through this." She cooed while stroking my hair. That was the most affection she had ever offered up to me in my entire life. I remember sinking deep into her arms thinking to myself, *what a DUMB BITCH—I should've killed her too.*

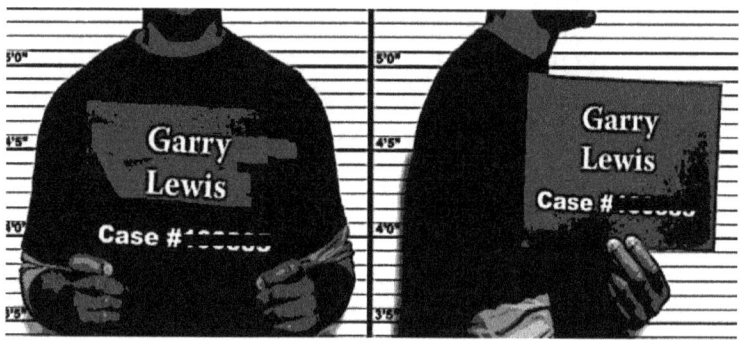

Chapter 7: Tooley's Hair & Nails

~Present Day 2016~

It's around 7AM and I just pulled up outside of my salon. That's right, *my very own* salon. It's still a surprise to me that I actually run my own business—and it's a successful one at that. For years once it opened, my shop was the only place in Tooley, Missouri where a woman could get her hair and nails done by professionals—so naturally I named it 'Tooley's Hair & Nails'. Of course after the city became more gentrified over the years, millions of other salons started opening up all over the place; though ours remained the most notable. Also fortunately for us, we serve some extremely loyal and satisfied customers who continuously come back to the shop with referrals; keeping us fairly unopposed.

I'm not going to sit here and say it's been my lifelong dream to do hair and nails, but what started out as a hobby and favor for close friends became something I could monetize. When I was a stripper a lot of the other dancers would see how I styled and maintained my own hair and nails and would beg me to do the same for them. I started charging for sessions once the demand for my services grew, and I decided to turn that little bit of momentum into this growing cash cow. I invested in myself and some of my stripper friends by putting all of us through cosmetology school—and the rest is history. Thank God for the sexual harassment lawsuit I won against my former employer in 2005; where I was granted five hundred thousand dollars. With that money I was able to put a down payment on the house Duggar and I currently live in, as well as purchase this decent sized store front.

~Flashback 2000~

William J. Hogan is a despicable man... but in my lifetime I've come across so many *despicable* men that to me, he is just another man. I met him when I was twenty-one-years-old in a hole-in-the-wall Dumois strip club called Sinsationals, where I used to dance. I was never one to keep up with tabloids so I had no idea who he was, the only thing I knew about him at the time was that he was very handsome for an old guy, and tipped AMAZINGLY. The other dancers were always jealous that he would constantly request dances from me, solely.

Back then Dixie and I had been Sinsationals' best dancers for over three years straight, so naturally we formed a bond over all the hate we received from the other girls. For working at an amateur ass strip club, the two of us had very impressive dance routines, plus it helped that our bodies were *and still are* phenomenal. Anyways, for weeks Hogan would come into Sinsationals and flirt with me heavily. He would always get pissy drunk and start telling me about how much he was worth (somewhere close to a billion dollars). Not to mention he also claimed to run one of the top law firms in North America, but I would always brush off his rants and view them as nothing more than intoxicated antics. After all, it *was* a strip club, and strip clubs are regularly filled with patrons who lie to get the adoration of their favorite dancers.

"I'm serious; I can't believe you've never heard of Hogan & Wildes, LLP! It's the most successful firm in Missouri!" He would boast.

"I'm not even from Missouri." I'd respond rolling my eyes.

"Oh really? I'm sorry, I just assumed you were like these other girls in here; Dumois rejects that have never once stepped foot outside this city." He laughed arrogantly.

"No… I grew up in Chicago. This is paradise compared to my old neighborhood. I'd rather be a reject in a poor, yet safe city than end up dead like my parents." I solemnly admitted.

"Damn girl, you sound like you've had a tough life. Is that why you're such a prude?" He joked.

"A prude?" I questioned him.

"Well Diamond *(which was my stripper name)*, I've fucked every girl in this club, but no matter how much attention and money I shower you with, you won't let me touch you." He whined. "I mean; I basically pay your rent but you won't even tell me your real name!"

"It's Jasmine, okay?" I responded rolling my eyes. "There are just way too many STD's out here that's why I just don't sleep with anyone. Plus, I don't like to sleep with my well-off clients… that would really just mess up business for me. Your money has been consistent and I don't want to fuck that up, you know?" I remember honestly informing him. "I've seen other guys have sex with other dancers and then come back in here acting way too clingy and way too crazy for my taste." Hogan suddenly spat out his alcohol and began laughing hysterically at my explanation even though I was being completely genuine. Plus, at that stage of my life, a man was the last thing on my list of needs. After all, four years prior to that moment I had to flee from Chicago due to the dysfunction in my last real relationship. My testimony was what put Killa away for life; so as far as I was concerned, men equaled trouble so making money became my sole priority.

"Tell you what—what if I became your boss, not just your client. Would you fuck me then?" He asked frankly.

"Oh so now you're a club owner and not just a lawyer?" I giggled at how preposterous he sounded.

"I meant… what if I gave you a job at my firm." He reiterated.

"Me? In a law firm? Man, your time is up." I cackled as I got up from his lap and began to exit the private room we were in.

"Thirty-five thousand dollars a year with plenty of room for advancement, benefits—health insurance and a 401k, a desk, *and* your dignity."

"What's all that?" I inquired skeptically as I sucked my teeth.

"What I can offer you if you work for me… tell you what, don't answer me right away, just go home first, google my firm, and when you see that my name is on the damn building you'll realize I'm a man of my word. You have sex with me once and I'll make sure the job is yours." He said sternly.

"… And what would I do at this law firm?" I scoffed, still rather skeptical.

"I don't know, but I'll find *somewhere* to place you. I know every patron that comes in this shit hole is broke and spends all their money at the bar. You make below minimum wage throwing away your dignity. Even St. Louis strippers get more money than this." That's when he handed me his business card. "Time to get your life together, I could be your meal ticket out of this reject lifestyle." Hogan then laughed, finished off his gin, slammed his empty glass on a side table, and grabbed his coat. "Call me when you come to your senses." He finished off his pitch as he walked out of the room, leaving me alone in deep thought.

That night when I got home I ran the idea by Dixie.

"WILLIAM HOGAN OFFERED YOU A JOB?" She barked.

"… So everything he said was real?" I whimpered.

"GIRL ARE YOU SLOW? WILLIAM J. HOGAN IS ONE OF THE RICHEST MEN IN MISSOURI!" She yelled.

"*Shh!*" I motioned, "lower your damn voice."

"GIRL-A! You better take advantage of that drunken ass offer! All the Dumois lames you've been fucking since you moved to this city have done NOTHING for you. This man has changed the lives of ALL his side joints. He even dated Cindy Simon the famous singer! That man is Hollywood and he's a rich ass lawyer!" I spent the rest of that night researching William J. Hogan and his law firm. I learned that not only was he worth over five hundred million dollars, but a lot of his former female employees had made something of themselves. It wasn't hard at all to make the decision to agree to his terms, plus I thought that maybe if I worked my ass he'd be so impressed I wouldn't even have to have sex with him at all.

I ended up calling Hogan back the next day and letting him know I was down for the job. A week before my interview I picked up books on what being a legal secretary entailed. I have always been a smart girl; I guess I acquired that attribute from my mother. Nothing in life has ever been too hard for me once I sincerely applied myself. I truly believe that if it wasn't for the death of my parents and the fact that I was raised by my trifling uncle, I would have been very successful with an easy ass life. Who knows? —I probably would have one day owned a law firm my damn self.

Anyways, the day of the interview arrived and I met with the head of HR, Lindsay Carmichael. I blew that interview out of the park. I knew a lot for only studying the aspects of the position for a week.

"Can I be frank with you, darling? You sure do know your stuff for being recommended by Bill." Ms. Carmichael complimented me. "With how fast he recommended you as Louisa's replacement, I thought you were just another one of his floozies."

She laughed at her own statement as I just sat there grinning indifferently—she was such an unprofessional bitch.

Months passed and I excelled in the position. I was also a little hopeful that Hogan had forgotten I owed him intercourse. Due to the opportunity I was given, I was able to quit stripping and actually start saving money towards a car. I was constantly surrounded by positive influences at the firm, one being my supervisor Britney Greene. Britney pushed a Mercedes Benz and would always talk about being engaged to a guy who owned his own business. They were also house-shopping at the time, which was a really big deal for me especially since she wasn't that much older than I was. I even learned that she grew up just two blocks away from where I lived with Dixie; the slummy part of Dumois. Truth is a lot of people at the firm had those same 'rags to riches' stories, which inspired me daily to pave my own way.

Britney and I became very close as she mentored me and taught me even more about the job. I was a really good friend to her, except for the fact that I never shared with her how I actually acquired the job. Hogan told me he told everybody that I had former law experience so I didn't want to make him look like a liar. Plus, I know damn well she would have judged me if I told her Hogan just handed me the job in exchange for sex. I deserved to be there as much as everyone else regardless of how I actually got there... I worked my BUTT off in the short period I was employed at the firm—but it was all for nothing because eventually the facade came to an end.

One morning after months of excelling as Hogan's assistant legal secretary, I received an email from him asking me to meet him in his office. I remember it like it was yesterday:

"You wanted to see me?" I said meekly as I knocked on his very expensive, imported, South African carved wooden door.

"Yea, come in." He answered. I walked in slowly as my stomach began turning. I had never really spoken to Hogan one on one since he hired me. I always intentionally avoided him because in the depths of my soul, I knew I owed him my body and I really didn't want to give it to him. Britney also shared with me a dark secret about her and Hogan's trip to DC, where he bartered her current position for sex. I could tell she regretted her actions so much that I began to fear my own deal with the man. "Don't you owe me something?" He asked getting straight to the point.

"Yes." I sighed. "But I've been working my ASS off. I really want this job. I'm always on time, I'm always staying late to complete tasks, I'm an extremely fast learner, and I just don't want to sleep with you and have all that compromised."

"Blah, blah, blah..." William mocked. "We had a deal; sex for the job, PERIOD! Do you know how many people want your job? It's what we agreed on, I'm not asking for anything more or less." He spat.

"Yea, but I would never want it to get out that I was only handed this position because I agreed to sleep with you." I grumbled.

"Don't flatter yourself I wouldn't tell anyone about it so the only way people would find out is if *you* told them. Plus, I only really want it one time; do you really think anyone is going to find out about us after only one damn time?" He pled his case.

"Bill, I just don't feel right about it at all." I repeated.

"Cool." He responded calmly and then refocused his attention to the paperwork on his desk. As I got up to dismiss myself and walk out of the room, I heard him add: "... And Ms. Hall... please clean out your desk." I remember my heart stopped, that was the very moment I realized William J. Hogan was a cold blooded man. Unfortunately, regardless of how I felt about him he was absolutely right, we *did* have a deal.

"Fine!" I threw his coldness back in his face. "If you want to fuck me so bad, let's fuck!" I recall immediately starting to strip down completely naked, throwing my work attire recklessly across the floor of his office. William's eyes immediately widened as he fell victim to my seductive curves. I doubt he expected the encounter to occur right there in his office, but if it was a show Hogan wanted... a show was what he was going to get!

"Now this is more like it!" He began to clumsily unzip his pants as I performed a mini strip tease that I had learned from my days at Sinsationals. I sexily moved my way towards him wearing nothing but my work heels. Once I was by his side, I began to shove my jiggly ass in his face before grinding it against his crotch. I shook my jiggly ass in his face once I got to him and then began grinding against his groin.

"You like how that feels, baby?" I moaned.

"Yea… Definitely… *Mmm*… I've been wanting some of that." He cooed.

"Do you have a condom?" I took the time out to ask because thanks to my Uncle Dennis I knew what it felt like to be burned.

"Yea." He rolled his eyes. "For a stripper you sure do have a lot of rules." As soon as he placed the condom on his dick I sat on it and began riding the shit out of him. "DAMN BABY, slow down… damn..." He moaned quietly in an attempt to not be discovered by the rest of the office.

"Shut the fuck up! This is what you wanted right? And your ass better not cum!" I commanded while clenching my tight pussy around his decent sized dick. I'm not even going to lie, if it wasn't for the fucked up principle of the matter, I would have fully enjoyed Hogan inside of me. For a man in his forties he sure was keeping up with me, lifting his body and assisting me with every stroke. I then began shoving my nipples into Hogan's mouth as I bounced faster up and down on his lap, my fat ass smacked against his thighs and my wet pussy leaked all the way down his dick. Just as soon as we both were about to cum, we heard someone abruptly open up his office door:

"Well there you are, you slut!" It was Britney screaming from the entrance of Hogan's office. I still to this day CAN NOT BELIEVE that I forgot to lock the damn door! Hogan immediately threw me off his lap as soon as I hit the floor I began scrambling for my clothes. "FUCK BOTH OF Y'ALL, I QUIT!" Britney continued her tantrum in disgust as she stormed off leaving the office door wide open. That's when a group of lawyers, co-workers, and people from the cleaning crew began to surround the door and look in on Bill and I.

"FUCK!" I said under my breath as I began to hear chatter and gasps surround us. I was right, I was completely fucked; both literally and figuratively. I got fired from the firm that same day; Hogan got nothing but a slap on the wrist since his name *was* on the outside of the building. Suddenly, my only chance at a better life was stripped away. I was so embarrassed and news spread all over town that I became known as the company sleaze.

    Thankfully five years later that reputation worked in my favor. In 2005 a class action lawsuit was filed against Hogan and his firm and I was approached by a lawyer to be the face of the suit. I was personally granted half a million dollars after me and thirteen other women won the case. My testimony of Quid Pro Quo harassment was the easiest *of all the women involved* to prove, since it *did* occur in front of the entire office resulting in plenty of witnesses. He used his power to pick me up from a strip club and hire me as his assistant legal secretary JUST so he could do me, then he threatened to fire me once I refused. That broke every equal opportunity/sexual harassment rule in the book giving us a fairly solid case. Britney never once let me explain what the situation was; she just took me sleeping with Hogan as me being shady towards her, which was never really the case. She never bothered to understand how devastating the incident was for me especially since she went through almost the exact same shit with Hogan. My lawyers even contacted her about joining the suit against him but Britney never returned our calls—that self-righteous bitch, she lost out on getting paid because she didn't want people to group her in with the hundreds of other Hogan side pieces involved in the case. The truth is I only fucked Hogan in order to map out a better life for myself which is the EXACT same reason she did too. The only difference between us is that I'm not afraid to own up to my fucking mistakes, whereas she tries to hide hers.

~Present Day 2016~
    Anyways not all things bad came from Hogan and me fucking; after all I am turning the key to my very own storefront.
    "What's up girl? We missed you yesterday!" Dixie my former roommate says as we both enter the shop. Dixie is who I put in charge of my salon, I made her store manager. She is my right hand woman—because of her I am able to call out for doctor visits, *like the one I took yesterday*, and still have the peace of mind that my business is in good hands.
    "Yea sorry, I just wasn't feeling good at all!" I laugh.

"Oh I thought you had killed Homeboy." She says extremely serious.

"Kill him? For what?" I ask.

"Bitch, the man had his side joint Miya come through here yesterday." She reveals to me in disbelief.

"WHAT?" I exclaim.

"Yea that's exactly how I reacted. That manly looking bitch had the nerve to come in here, have ME style her hair and nails not knowing who she was and then on her way out she said *'tell Jasmine Miya was here, and I won't only have Duggar soon but I'll have this shop too.'* I would have gone upside her head but she jolted out the shop fast as hell. I know what the bitch looks like now so it won't ever happen again."

"Those damn two are getting HELLA disrespectful. I got something for Calvin's ass when I get home! Him and his little side bitch."

Chapter 8: A Shot at Love

~Flashback 2005~

  The reason I put up with Calvin "Homeboy" Duggar's bullshit is because he saved my life. After the first time we met at his concert five years back (when he and his boys gang banged me), I COMPLETELY lost respect for him as a man. I took down all his posters from my bedroom wall, and I threw out all of his CD's. I even got Dixie to start hating him right along with me, so it came as a shock to the both of us when we found out that he would be hosting a party at Sinsationals. After getting fired from Hogan & Wildes, LLP in the year 2000, and before I collected that large lump sum from the lawsuit I won against them, I had gone right back to stripping.

  Five years earlier I would have been ecstatic that Duggar was hosting a party at our little shit hole of a club. I would have been devising a master plan that would have made me stand out over the other girls because back then I wanted nothing more than to meet Homeboy Duggar. I wanted badly to develop a genuine connection with him, and also tell him how much his music influenced my life. Five years earlier I would have given him my body, soul, and mind—but because of how he treated me *like a fucking blow up doll* on the initial night we met, I was heartbroken and lost all adoration for him.

  When the night of the infamous party finally arrived, all the other dancers in the club were acting so extra and treating him like he was royalty. Women were pushing and shoving for his attention, but to me he was yesterday's news. I wanted nothing to do with him and I didn't care how much money he was dropping on stage, so I stayed my sexy ass in a corner. I spent most of the night away from the spotlight, and danced for the more low-key ballers in attendance. Sinsationals had never before seen a crowd like the one Duggar brought out and I honestly think that was his way of giving back to his little Dumois community. He could have been hosting parties at King of Diamonds or Stadium or other nationally acclaimed strip clubs, but there he was in his little forgotten city, bringing some shine to it. Even though I hated him at that moment, I do remember thinking his actions were rather commendable.

The night of the party, big spenders were definitely in full affect and my girls were visibly ecstatic. Aside from Dixie and I, not many of the other dancers at Sinsationals made up to a hundred dollars on a *good* night, so this additional cash flow was raising everybody's spirits. As for me, I was grateful for the extra money but after fucking a millionaire like Hogan, and seeing all the things he could do for me, I stopped being impressed by rich entertainers in lower tax brackets.

After the great night ended, I packed up all my belongings, waited with the other girls as the patrons cleared out and then began to make my way home. (Most of us Sinsationals dancers didn't have cars and lived in section eight developments that were practically walking distances from the club. So what we girls normally did was wait out in the locker-room for the club to empty out before leaving; a safety precaution that helped us avoid being followed home or harassed by neurotic patrons). That's why I was nearly startled to death when as I crossed the street of the club, I heard someone yell out after me.

"Hey ma, wait up!" The person hollered. It was dark as hell and I didn't want to wait around to see who it was so I ignored the voice and began speed walking. I've had crazy stalkers before so I assumed this situation was no different. "HOLD UP YO!" The voice got increasingly aggressive and was less than a few feet behind me so I turned around abruptly, firmly grasping the bottle of pepper spray I had in my purse.

"DO NOT TAKE ANOTHER STEP!" I commanded. That's when I realized the stranger behind me had been Duggar all along. "What the hell are you still doing here?" I scolded him, my fear immediately turning to anger. "You scared me half to death!".

"Damn, you're a little feisty one, huh?" He laughed off the disrespect. "Usually strippers are happy to be around Homeboy Duggar, I guess that's not the case for you." He laughed, cockily referring to himself in first person.

"How are you just walking around this neighborhood at four in the morning? Aren't you way too famous for this shit?" I scoffed.

"My tour bus is just around the corner ma, and I actually waited for you to get off work so I could ask if you needed a ride home." He offered. "One of the dancers told me you didn't drive.

I've been out here for over two hours, you all take forever packing up."

"Man..." I snickered off his kind gesture and kept walking towards the house Dixie and I shared.

"*Man* what?" Duggar asked shocked by my blatant rejection—Lord knows what it must have done to his enormous ego.

"I'm not interested." I coldly reiterated and then turned and walked away.

"How do you know? —so you really won't even give me a chance?" He called after me.

"OH I KNOW!" I deviously chuckled as I turned back around and stormed towards him. "You really don't remember me do you?" I questioned him in disbelief.

"Remember you? Uh... No... *Should I?*" Duggar looked confused.

"We've already had sex, you idiot! It happened after your Tooley concert five years ago. You and your entourage gang banged me! Well... technically you were the only one that I let penetrate me, but I pleasured the other guys with my mouth and hands." I bluntly and sarcastically admitted.

"Oh shit!" Duggar is caught off guard by my frankness. "Honestly I've fucked so many groupies I really, *really* don't remember... NOT SAYING YOU'RE A GROUPIE OR ANYTHING, I'm just actually really disappointed in myself that I didn't take down your number back then. I was probably drunk or high because I would have never given up on a body like yours with a sound mind. I loved EVERYTHING I saw tonight even though you were so far away from me giving everyone else attention BUT me. I really loved what I saw, and I would really like to take you out."

"Save all that game for your mama." I spewed. "You had your chance back in 2000 and you blew it! I damn near loved you, you were my whole world and you had sex with me and then tossed me to the side like a pile of garbage." I unwillingly began to cry. I had no idea at the time how strong my feelings for Duggar still were.

"Damn, ma. I was messed up back then. Don't tell me I lost a fan off that dumb shit. Listen, I have back to back shows here in the area for the next two days. Do you mind if I come back here to see you?" He turned on the charm so well and asked ever so politely that I couldn't resist.

"Okay... I guess." I decided to let the past go, after all what was I really mad at? The fact that a rapper didn't make me his wife after I gave it up to him in front of his whole entourage the first night I met him? Ha! At least he didn't remember me in that light and I had a second chance at first impressions.

"It's a date then." He smiled and then kissed me on the forehead before getting back on his tour bus. That night I ended up practically floating the rest of my way home, as mad as I once was at Duggar, who knew all it would take was a little bit of conversation to mend things. I loved Duggar before I ever met him, even more than I ever lusted after Edmond, my elementary school crush, or Killa, my first real boyfriend—what I felt for Duggar was different, and it had ABSOLUTELY NOTHING to do with his financial status and popularity. I just really, really related to his music. He touched my soul, and now the universe was giving him and me a second chance at love. Duggar stuck to his word and came back on both the following nights, unpaid, just to see me—a beautiful sentiment then, but looking back now I wish he would have just stayed the hell away from me.

I let Calvin into the locker room the second night he was at Sinsationals and he didn't even try to sleep with me. We just stayed backstage talking until really late waiting for the club to clear out. He even ended up walking me all the way home; his entourage trailing closely behind from their tour bus. It was all so romantic. We both were amazed at how easily our conversations flowed and how quickly we developed feelings for one another... everything just fit.

"I'm going to be honest; yesterday I just wanted to fuck you when I stopped you, but after tonight... I'm trying to actually get to know you on a personal level." He genuinely revealed.

"Whatever, you're just telling me anything." I chuckled. "As soon as I give it up to you, all this special treatment you've been giving me will be gone."

"Really? You still think I'm a dog, huh? GIRL THAT WAS FIVE YEARS AGO! I'm a new man! Had enough groupies to last a lifetime, now I'm in my mid-thirties with dreams of finding a real shorty like you to settle down with." He sincerely expressed.

"*Riiiiight.*" I responded, a bit skeptical.

"Okay stop!" He ordered with frustration in his voice. "What do I have to do to prove to you that I'm serious about starting a real relationship with you?"

"I think you've been shot by Cupid's bow because you're not acting very 'rapper like', Mr. Duggar." I snickered. That's when he ran to his tour bus and began climbing to the top of it; his road team watched in fear from the inside.

"Don't fucking break your legs, Homeboy!" His manager snarled out of one of the windows. Duggar's bodyguards then surrounded the side of the bus he was climbing up on, ready to catch him in case he toppled down. Once at the very top of the bus, Calvin stood close to the edge and spread out his arms like he was Rose from the movie 'Titanic' in the *I'm flying* scene and yelled out:

"I, CALVIN 'HOMEBOY' DUGGAR, AM FALLING DANGEROUSLY IN LOVE WITH THIS GIRL RIGHT HERE NAMED DIAMOND!" I rolled my eyes because the man didn't even use my real name. I told him what it was the day before but he probably already forgot it. Diamond was my stripper name; how could he claim to love a girl whose real name he didn't even know. "I LOVE JASMINE *DIAMOND* HALL!" He added just before all hope was lost.

Woah, I thought to myself, *he remembered... he must really like me.* I was completely sold on him at that point. It was around five o'clock in the morning when we finally reached my house, luckily for Duggar the hood was asleep by then; otherwise it would've been pandemonium in my housing area over the infamous rapper's presence. He passionately kissed me goodnight and we went our separate ways. He didn't ask to come inside or anything, he was a perfect gentleman and that was how he won me over completely for the second time.

Now that third and final night at Sinsationals was the night that changed both of our lives forever. I was a guest at Duggar's VIP table and cuddled up beside him as if we had been a couple for years. The public display of affection at the club showed me that he really did change and really was serious about a relationship with me. The fact that he was a famous rapper but treated a lowly stripper like myself passionately in public told me everything I needed to know about his intentions. He wanted me as much as I wanted him even though his PR was in his ear telling him a relationship with me would be bad for business. Duggar wasn't the only one taking some heat for our relationship; ALL the other dancers at Sinsationals, INCLUDING Dixie, witnessed the blossoming love between him and me and became extremely jealous. Luckily we both didn't care what the naysayers thought; we were way too busy floating off on cloud nine—until:

CLICK CLACK the sound of a cocking gun was heard not too far from my head.

When I looked up to see where the noise was coming from, I was staring down a barrel pointed directly at me less than two feet away. That's when chaos ensued and people started screaming and running out of the club. Even the music abruptly stopped and the DJ was nowhere to be found, but Duggar stayed very still and calmly remained by my side. I took a good look at the man aiming his weapon at me but for the life of me I couldn't recognize him. He had two men who were also armed standing next to him, though he was the only one with his weapon drawn.

"Hey Puma… Isn't that the bitch that got us set up in Chi-town?" The gunman shouted to one of his companions.

"Yea, that's the fucking bitch!" The second man cosigned. "The hotel in Chicago… She tricked us and got us robbed. YO IT'S DEFINITELY HER CHICO!" Immediately Duggar and I were surrounded by about ten other men. They even held guns to the temples of each of Duggar's body guards.

"Robbing us was the dumbest shit you ever did BITCH! Your man at the time, *Killa*, should have done his research. We're the Latos gang from East LA; we have connections in EVERY hood which means we're NOT to be fucked with. You pussies thought shit was sweet because we were from out of town, huh? Well after that shit went down, because of our vast connections we found out exactly who you guys were in less than a week. Found out Killa and his boys, *fortunately for them,* are locked up, and we searched far and wide for your ass in Chicago… but you were missing in action, I guess hiding out in this shit hole. Trust and believe when your man gets out we'll gun him and his crew down one by one, but we got something for you in the meantime, you're about to eat this bullet right here." Duggar was lost and didn't understand what was going on, but I knew my past had just, at this very moment, caught up with my ass. These were some of the men Killa and I had set up and robbed back in my teenage years in Chicago. At that moment the man had his gun aimed directly towards my heart and he was just about to squeeze the trigger and abruptly end my life. What happened in the next five seconds changed my life forever, as I froze and screamed covering up my face with my arms, the gun went off and I felt Duggar leap in front of me; shielding me from harm. His well-trained bodyguards then followed suit and suddenly attacked the Latos gang members, gaining control of all their weapons and causing them to flee the club. I grabbed a hold of Duggar when all was safe; extremely thankful to be alive and relieved to hear police sirens in the near distance.

"You saved my life!" I cried to him. "Duggar?" I shook him when I realized he wasn't responding. That's when I noticed he had been shot. I noticed blood gushing from his drenched pant leg splashing EVERYWHERE and flowing on to the floor. Before that night I had never smelled or seen that much blood in my life. He had become unconscious and was barely breathing by the time paramedics got to him. Thankfully Calvin ultimately survived that night, and after the whole ordeal I had zero doubt as to whether or not Calvin loved me. I realized what he felt for me was unconditional and that no one other than my birth parents had ever made me feel as secure and wanted as he did. *No greater love than he who lays down his life...*

Unfortunately, Duggar's music career took a nose dive after the leg injury he incurred. A shot straight to his shin was enough to leave him in a wheelchair for almost an entire decade. It would be years after that before he ever walked again. That's why I vowed to stay by his side forever, through the thick and the thin—and I've been doing exactly that ever since.

~Present Day 2016~

"I don't know why the hell she came to your shop, Jas. You know damn well I would never have disrespected you in that way,

EVER!" Calvin screams at me at the top of his lungs. "You really think that after ALL we've been through together, after ALL we shared that I would tell a little side hoe to come to your shop and demean you? Man… you've got me fucked up!" He was right. We both obviously had a problem controlling our side situations. Here I was pregnant with my side dude, and Duggar's side bitch was disrespecting me not knowing her place as the side bitch that she was.

"I'm going to let this moment slide, but the next time she comes out of pocket you can get the hell out of my house!" I say threatening him, even though I've been using that same peril since 2005. "I mean it this time! Or else I'm going to get that bitch touched!" I add.

Duggar knew a lot about my past, including that I was a three-time killer. He knew I wasn't bluffing and that the-old-me would ruin that Miya chick if she ever tried it with me again. Duggar and I kept each other's deep dark secrets. Just like he knew about my trials and tribulations, I knew about his…

~Flashback 1982~

Duggar was around twelve years old when he began to feel "confused". The effects of the abuse he encountered with the teenage boy who molested him four years earlier began to surface. He told me about one instance when he was running around with his cousin of the same age and they were playing in the mud. His mother told them to go get cleaned up and the two preteens ran inside and started stripping naked to shower together. It wasn't unusual for the two, who were extremely close and had showered together since birth, to hop in the tub together to save time. They would even play the adolescent game of innocently slapping each other's dicks.

The only difference is, in that instance after they were naked in the shower and his cousin jokingly and non-sexually slapped his dick—Calvin instantly became fully erect. "WHAT THE FUCK? BOY YOU'RE GAY!" He remembered his cousin screaming to him as he angrily exited the shower. "I'M NEVER PLAYING WITH YOUR GAY ASS AGAIN!" After that day Duggar lost the companionship of his closest family member, he still cries about that very moment. He had always been only attracted to girls, so what happened that day in the shower was foreign and confusing to him.

    I reassured Duggar that he wasn't gay. Since that horrific day Duggar's dick has never again gotten hard from another male. I honestly think he was just going through puberty and his body was confused, I also think the abuse he encountered at an earlier age played a role in that moment. I kept his secret and I never lost any respect for him. We are one in the same him and I. I sometimes looked at women with mixed feelings too. I think when you've been abused as a child your sexual compass goes haywire. I don't identify as gay, but sometimes I have unexplainable thoughts. Now I'm not saying only abused children turn out becoming gay or having gay tendencies—I work in a salon for Pete's sake, I have too many gay men employed under me to think that naively. I know most gays are born gay—but there are a few of us, curious/emotionally damaged people, who were *made* not born. Duggar would never sleep with a man, just like I would never chase after pussy… I know we both seem like hella-fucked-up people—but in our defense we've both been dealt fairly fucked up hands. We'll get through it though…together. I love him and he loves me and that's really all that matters.

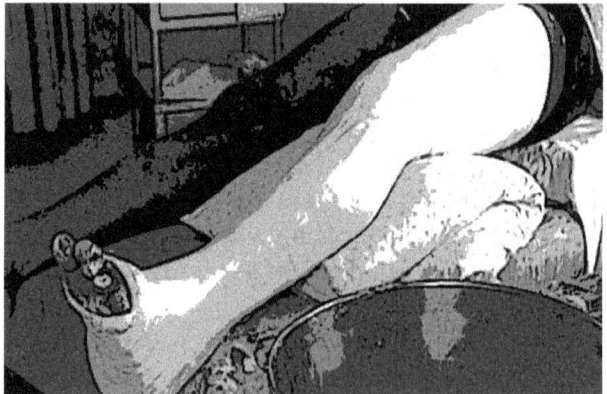

Chapter 9: Best Served Cold

~Present Day 2016~

I wake up nauseous and speedily run to the bathroom—morning sickness is the worst part of being pregnant. I know these symptoms far too well; after all, I was once pregnant before, at age fourteen. I'm extremely grateful to have Dixie in my life, because of how great she is at managing my shop; I am able to take all the days off that I need. I also do most of my supply ordering online anyways, so having a great laptop at home helps me manage as well... besides it's not like doing hair and nails is a passion of mine.

I think it's hilarious that Dixie still has no idea I'm even pregnant and believes that every time I call out it has to do with Calvin's infidelity. She has no idea Duggar and I have an extremely open relationship. I enjoy the fact that she doesn't know everything that goes on in my life. I have nothing against the girl, and she's never given me a reason not to trust her, it's just that Britney has taught me not to put anything past a female—they're rather venomous.

Duggar is sound asleep next to me, snoring. I can't help but stare at him, even though he's getting older and he's not in the best shape of his life, he's still an extremely handsome man. I know why he's sleeping so peacefully; he thinks I'm going to abort this baby growing inside of me today. The truth is, I would never get rid of this amazing gift I've been given. Even though this is Jeremy's baby, I'm pretty sure Duggar and I can come together and raise it as if it were our own. I know Duggar's not going to leave me anyways, who else is going to put up with all his bullshit and vice versa? We're two peas in a pod him and I.

~Flashback to Three Months Earlier~

I was at Morehouse Coffee Shop ordering a pumpkin latte. I always stopped there after work since it's located on my way home from the salon. I'm weird, unlike most people who like their coffee in the mornings; I prefer my cups at night. I also like to add a lot of liquor in my coffee so drinking that mix in the morning would be counterproductive. The alcohol goes perfectly with the Morehouse blend I love and always gives it an extra kick. I keep a medium sized flask in my purse; it helps me deal with my super long work days and PTSD (acquired from the various disturbing experiences from my past). Anyways, I was sitting there minding my own damn business when someone aggressively patted me on my shoulder.

"It's you isn't it?" The voice said from behind me, turning around I saw that it was Jeremy Rogers, and I jumped. The last time I saw that man was almost eleven years prior and we didn't exactly leave on a good note.

"Yea, it's me." I smirked.

"Ivy—right?" He asked, not at all amused.

"Yep, I love that you remembered the name I gave you almost eleven years ago."

"Did you follow me back to my home town?" Jeremy ignored my statement and became visibly concerned.

"Don't flatter yourself." I scoffed as I rolled my eyes and turned back around to enjoy my spiked coffee. I was already somewhat buzzed and I didn't need that goody two-shoes fucking up my high. "You might be the one following me, what the fuck is a millionaire like yourself doing so close to the tracks?" I laughed at my statement but it didn't make it any less true. The part of Tooley we were in hadn't been renovated yet. The Morehouse Coffee Shop was literally a block away from the city train tracks so technically I was in *my* neck of the woods, whereas Jeremy was hours away from his home in Uptown Tooley.

"This will always be my home no matter how much money I make or how far I move away. I was born and raised in Dumois, *unlike you*. I can tell you're an outsider by your accent. Also, a lot of the money I'VE donated to charity has ended up on THESE very streets. So if you *must* know I'm here on business… but why am I explaining myself to you anyways? I still think you're a nut job." He spewed at me in a demeaning 'know-it-all' tone.

"No, Jeremy… You're just an idiot!" I fired right back at him. That's when Jeremy uninvitingly sat himself right across from me. Truth was I gave up on my revenge plan when I waited over a decade for him to call me after that crazy night at the Ritz-Carlton. I hate rejection and the fact that he never took advantage of being able to have his way with me made me question his sexuality entirely. As far as I was concerned, he and Britney deserved each other. I washed my hands clean and vowed to stay clear of the Rogers' forever, so seeing him again just brought back the bitterness I thought I had gotten over.

"Look…" I began.

"NO—YOU look. Over ten years ago you snuck into *my* hotel room in DC and got naked in front of me and tried to seduce me, making some very harsh accusations towards my wife. What the fuck was that about?" He barked.

"You weren't interested then, so why the fuck do you care so much about it now?" I interjected.

"It definitely matters now especially since you're in my fucking home town! The Ritz security thought we were together, they said you tied up one of their employees! I almost got fucking locked up in DC for abetting a kidnapper. I told them you were staying with Homeboy Duggar but he told the police his guest had been with him the entire night so I looked delusional. They didn't believe me when I told them I had no fucking clue who you really were. At first sight I thought you were just a horny groupie, but now I think you're obviously bat shit crazy. What are the chances that ten years later you're in a fucking coffee shop in my hometown? How do I trust that you're not still following me around with some crazy ass intensions? I'm just looking out for the safety of my family now because this has gone too far, so I'm going to need some answers." He disgorged; Jeremy was so naïve it made me sick.

"I LIVE in Tooley, *genius*. And I wasn't lying about being a guest of Homeboy Duggar's, YOU SAW ME WITH HIM AT THE TABLE THE FIRST HALF OF THE GALA! Truth is I'm his girlfriend and we have a house here! No one is worried about your little fake ass happy family." I retorted.

"Girlfriend? —then how come back then you said he was your cousin?"

"I lied."

"Well what the hell else did you lie to me about that night?"

"My name…" I laughed.

"I'm glad you find all this very amusing. You scared the hell out of me with your antics." He sternly informed me.

"Look, I was just trying to fuck with you and your wife that night. I'm over it. I'm a business owner now; I have a lot going for myself… I'm really over it—ALL!" I informed him brushing him off attempting to get back to my spiked cup of Joe.

"What did you have against, Britney? Why go through those great lengths to sleep with me?"

"Your wife is a piece of shit." I responded bluntly.

"Wow. Okay… rather harsh considering that you don't even know her."

"That's the one thing I didn't lie about Mr. Rogers. I know your damn wife, probably better than you know her yourself." I scoffed.

"Oh really?" He asked suspiciously.

"Yea… We used to work together at Hogan & Wildes." I revealed.

"Well what the hell did she do to you?"

"She judged me." I replied honestly.

"Judged you? So that's reason enough to break into her husband's hotel room and try to seduce him, and tie up a fucking maid?"

"Yes." I said coldly, and then refocused my attention outside.

"Explain." He insisted.

"I don't owe you an explanation… besides, like I said… I'm over it."

"Explain… *please*." That's when I looked deep into Jeremy's eyes and saw something in them I had never seen before—pure weakness. I immediately began to pity him. If Britney is anything like Duggar and I *(which she most definitely is)* and Jeremy really is the '*good guy*' he portrays to be, then he's in some deep shit right now. People like me don't know how to love; all we do is break hearts. The openness Duggar and I share is rare and the only way a twisted relationship like ours ever works is if both parties are completely honest with each other—unfortunately not everyone is comfortable sharing their loved one with someone else and also people tend to lack the strength to accept and dish out such brutal honesty. "Look… I can't believe I'm confiding in you but… Do you know anything about a guy named Adam?" He asked breaking the awkward silence.

"No. Why?"

"Never mind, forget that I brought it up." He exhaled heavily.

"No—tell me. What's up Jeremy?" I sincerely inquired.

"My wife and I—Britney—were at a restaurant weeks ago and our server was this man in his mid-thirties. He was so excited to see my wife, Like OVERLY excited. And I'm just sitting there like *dude, chill*! She brushed the whole ordeal off and claimed that he was just some former fast food employee that worked at a chain across the street from her old job. Since that day I haven't been able to suppress my feelings of suspicion."

"Did she say the guy worked at the Burger Royale?" I asked, holding back laughter.

"Yea, so you know him?" He asked eagerly.

"Yea, that's the Burger Royale boy. Britney told me all about him years ago. She and I used to be really close for the short time I knew her. She's definitely fucked him in the past."

"Oh." Sadness immediately took over his entire disposition.

"Yep, they fucked right over there." I pointed outside of the Morehouse window to the Vacation Inn. "They were regulars there; she fucked him almost every weekend for six months while you were engaged. She even told me he was a better lover than you were, she liked his aggressiveness. She told me she thought he was beautiful but that he had obvious gold-digging tendencies that turned her off. I bet you if he didn't use her all the time she probably would have left you for him." I decided to be as blunt as possible because I felt like the man had been lied to enough times.

"God… That guy must've barely been eighteen back then. What the fuck is wrong with her?" He asked having gloom written all over his face.

"That's what I was trying to tell you years ago back in DC. Look, Britney is *just* like me, except I'm as real as they get. She ended our friendship because she thought I was a hoe when in reality she did the exact same shit I did. I thought that was very hypocritical of her." I explained.

"So you cheat on Duggar?" Jeremy asked prying in my business.

"Yes, we both cheat, and we're both brutally honest about it." I admitted.

"I don't want an open marriage with my wife; I already had to share her earlier on in our relationship." He explained. "Do you think she's still fucking that burger kid Adam?"

"I don't know, but when it comes to people like Britney and I… we hardly ever change." I scrupulously replied. Immediately after I spoke, what I never ever in my lifetime expected to happen, did; Jeremy burst out into tears. Damn, here I thought he was the enemy when in reality we were both on the same side. We've both been hurt by Britney, just in different ways. He wasn't the enemy—*she* was.

"Stop it. Here, have some of this." I said handing him my secret stash of liquor. He took the flask to the head and almost downed my entire supply. "Woah, slow down buddy!" I laughed, fairly impressed with his drinking abilities. "You don't even know what's in there!"

"I don't care; I need something to numb this pain. Hey, can we get out of here? I could use another drink and this is almost empty." He asked. At that point I think Jeremy also realized we were more kin-like than foe.

"Bet." I responded. That night we ended up going to a hole in the wall bar across the street from the coffee shop. We both drank A LOT. We started exchanging war stories and comparing notes on Britney's behavior. From what I heard from Jeremy, it seemed like Britney hadn't changed a bit in all those years. I let him know about everything Britney had ever told me about their relationship and her past even though my information was seventeen years old, he found it very useful.

"I think she's cheating again… I... I really do. I gave her my fucking all from the very beginning. We have two kids together! Right after we first got married it was all good, she told me almost everything. Then random guys started popping back up in her text messages and she even stopped going to church. I don't know if I can handle being screwed over again, I'm a good fucking guy. Women hit on me, I mean GORGEOUS women. For God's sake YOU were even BUTT NAKED in my hotel room—READY! And I rejected you for HER! If she's out here doing me dirty, I'M DONE, I'm really, really done this time!" He explained, slurring every other word. I don't know if it was because of the alcohol, but Jeremy suddenly began getting really loose and looking particularly handsome; sexier than I remembered him in DC.

"No one deserves to be treated like that; I agree you are a very faithful man… because honey, even I wouldn't have been able to resist all this ass." I said as I hopped off of the bar stool I was seated in and began to grab and jiggle my own ass. That's when I noticed his facial expression changed from sorrow-filled to lustful. At that moment I knew exactly what was on his mind—Jeremy wanted to fuck me. Catching his gawking eyes made him blush and then immediately turn away.

"I'm sorry, I should be getting home." He said while abruptly getting up from his own bar stool.

"Are you sure?" I gently tugged on his arm, bringing his hand up close to my plump lips. "You sure there's nothing I can help you with before you head home?" I asked seductively as I took his entire pointer finger into my mouth. I began clenching my juicy lips around it and groping his finger hungrily with my tongue.

"Oh shit." I heard him exhale with pleasure. At this point we were both wasted out of our minds.

"Do you want to go get a room right next door at the Vacation Inn?" I asked him getting straight to the point. After having that hour long eye-opening discussion about Britney, all those old feelings of revenge resurfaced. I realized that night was probably the last time I would ever get Jeremy that drunk and open with me, so I decided to relaunch my plan of revenge against his wife. I was going to fuck Jeremy, record the whole ordeal on camera, and then send the video to his wife—the DC plan was back in full effect.

"I don't know…" Jeremy responded, clearly torn between cheating and executing his own revenge towards his whore of a wife.

"THAT BITCH HURT THE BOTH OF US! Let's get a fucking room, have the best sex of our lives and then go our separate ways. With all the grimy shit she's done to you, you are entitled to mess up at least once. I swear ONE time, and you'll never hear from me again."

"Okay." He agreed quicker than I expected him to. I was so shocked and excited I began doing cartwheels in my mind.

Jeremy and I paid the balance on our tab and drunkenly stumbled out of the bar. With our cars still parked in front of Morehouse Coffee Shop we wobbled our way over to the Vacation Inn. After booking our hotel room, once finally inside our animalistic nature took over. I no longer recognized the timid, meek man I was just having drinks with. Jeremy suddenly turned into a brute and began man-handling me; it was as if he was in a drunken rage. He even ripped off his shirt without bothering to unbutton it; I was definitely taken off guard.

"Woah, dude, calm down." I said a little intimidated.

"Shut the fuck up!" Jeremy ordered. Then he threw me on one of the double beds in the grungy hotel room. "Take it all off." He commanded. I must admit that, that new side of Jeremy was very scary and extremely sexy at the same time.

"Who the hell are you talking to?" I responded with a fake attitude. Jeremy ignored me and shoved me around a little while ripping off my own clothes. Once I was completely naked he swiftly turned me over onto my knees, gripped a handful of my curly hair, and jerked my head as far back as it could go, all the while guiding himself deep into my already wet pussy.

"OOOOH!" I shouted. He was surprisingly bigger than most men I'd been with in the past, so I immediately felt that initial stroke deep inside of my gut. With complete disregard for my pain, Jeremy continued to pull my hair and plummet deeper inside of me, over and over again. "I CAN'T BABY, I CAN'T TAKE IT!" I screamed.

"CALL ME DADDY!" He ordered.

"DADDY I CAN'T, PLEASE DADDY, I CAN'T… SLOW DOWN!" I yelled as every stroke got more intense. "I'M ABOUT TO CUM DADDY! I'M ABOUT TO CUM ON YOUR DICK!" I screamed as my body just let go. My pussy began to throb around his hard dick, but he still didn't stop. "I can't baby… I can't… please cum already." I pleaded. Half an hour went by and Jeremy was still carrying on at the same pace; fucking my brains out. The man had the type of stamina I had never experienced before, I think he was taking out on me all the built up aggression he had towards his wife.

"I'm not going to stop baby; I love this pussy. You came and I didn't get to cum yet. That's not fair is it? I'm trying to take my time and remember this pussy since it's my last time in it. Please don't make me stop." He begged me which turned me on all over again. "Are you going to ride it for daddy?" He asked.

"Yes baby." I obliged, giving in. Jeremy then got on his back and waited for me to mount him. Right before I got on top I began to do some extremely kinky shit and lick off my own juices from his penis.

"Oh shit." He moaned with pleasure. "Yesss!" It turned me on to be able to reciprocate the pleasure he gave to me just a few moments earlier.

"You like that daddy?" I teased him while his penis was still deep inside of my mouth.

"I love it, I love it. I love you." He let slip. That's when I began to lose my mind.

"You love me?" I asked, somewhat in a trance.

"Yes, I love you so much. I love how you make me feel." He reassured me. I stopped sucking his dick and suddenly moved my lips from his groin area to his stomach, then ended up at his chest. I hesitated because I knew normally guys like him didn't like to kiss girls like me. At that moment I began to feel really emotional. I still couldn't believe he said he loved me. Before I made an initial move, Jeremy unexpectedly pulled me up to his lips and planted a kiss on my own lips. I remember thinking it was the most passionate a man had ever kissed me, his tongue practically made love to mine. He never once made me feel cheap or disgusting like almost every other man I'd ever slept with in the past had made me feel. Even the love of my life, Duggar, had me feeling cheap after our very first sexual encounter. Jeremy was different; he treated me like a queen the first time in that hotel room. That's why I mounted his dick like a stallion and rode him like he was the last dick I would ever have inside of me; all while he kissed me passionately. I bounced on his penis so fast he started clenching onto the sheets on the bed. "DAMN GIRL!" He moaned.

"You like my pussy daddy?" I cooed.

"I LOVE THAT SHIT!" He exclaimed. "I love it so much I want to taste it!" He immediately carried me off of his dick and laid me on my back. He hungrily spread my legs and began to eat my pussy frantically.

"FUCK!" I cried as I ran my fingers through his soft curly mane. "I'm about to cum AGAIN! Damn daddy, what the fuck are you doing to me?" I cried. Before he could respond something crazy happened, I began to squirt. The reason that was such a big deal was because I had never before squirted in my entire life and until that night I thought squirting was just something people made up or some special effects porn producers created—but boy was I wrong.

"That's right baby DAMN, I have never seen anybody squirt in real life." He said sounding just as excited as I was. Embarrassed, I tried to bury my head inside the covers. "Nah, don't be embarrassed, that shit was sexy as hell. You're like my sexual soulmate. It's going to be hard never fucking you again." He admitted. "Can I have some more please or is it too sensitive?'

"It's sensitive but I still want to." I admitted.

"Okay, then I'll go slowly this time." He promised and then slowly reinserted himself inside of me. Even his slow strokes were just as intense as the fast ones. *God*, I remember thinking, *this is the best sex I've ever had.* Immediately after that thought Jeremy said, "Damn, this is the BEST pussy I've ever had." From there we both started to lose our minds. The initial pain I felt from the continuous fucking disappeared as my pussy got wetter than it's ever been. All I wanted to do was make him cum. I grabbed his buttocks while guiding him deeper and deeper inside of me; winding my hips and grinding against his groin area with each stroke. He lasted for about three more minutes before I felt him explode deep inside of my pussy. Seeing him go crazy with pleasure caused me to reach yet another climax of my own.

Jeremy Rogers made me cum three times that night, which was a record high. And because of that beautiful night, I am now three months pregnant with his child. I remember every aspect of that incident and for the past couple of months I've been dying to relive it over and over again—actually thanks to the fact that I had hidden my camera phone on a shelf in the hotel room and recorded the entire ordeal without any suspicions from Jeremy, I would always have a memory of that moment… and one day so would his wife.

~Flashback 1994~

Like I said, I've been pregnant once before. I was fifteen years old when I found out and it was Uncle Dennis' child. It was without question that I decided to get rid of his demon child so at the time an abortion was the only option. I remember skipping school and going to the clinic myself using a fake ID a classmate had loaned me that said I was eighteen years old. Some people consider abortion to be murder; well if that is in fact the case then Dennis' baby was the first out of three people I have murdered in my lifetime (Dennis being the second). I don't regret either act one bit; I would kill them both again in a heartbeat if I had to.

Chapter 10: Closeted

~Present Day 2016~

"When are you getting rid of that thing?" Calvin spews out of nowhere. The two of us are lying in bed catching up on the latest ratchet reality TV series.

"Get rid of what?" I blurt out, my guilt rather conspicuous. I know damn well what he is referring to... *my baby*. "Do we have to talk about this now Cal? This is a really funny episode." I laugh off the awkwardness of the conversation and refocus my attention to the television. Duggar immediately hops out of bed and limps over to the TV (which is mounted on our wall); he then dramatically turns it off manually. "Jeez, Calvin, what the fuck?" I sigh.

"Exactly Jasmine, what in the flying fuck? It's been a month since you told me you were pregnant, what are you now? A good four months along? You need to go and get that shit taken care of." He aggravatingly whines.

"Baby, we need to talk..."

"Don't. DO NOT even *baby* me. Are you—are you really considering going through with this fucking pregnancy?" Duggar's voice cracks in the middle of that last statement and I can tell he is close to tears. I get out of the bed and run to his side to console him. No matter how dysfunctional the two of us are together, I love this man with my entire soul.

"I just was thinking you know, with us never being able to have children of our own, that this baby would be good for us."

"GOOD FOR *US*? YOU'RE GOING TO HAVE ANOTHER MAN'S CHILD? REALLY? HOW IN THE WORLD IS THAT IN ANY WAY GOOD FOR US?" At this point his tears are visibly streaming down the side of his face.

"No, I'm going to have OUR child." I coo.

"*OUR* child? Man you know DAMN well I can't make babies, that child is whatever dude you've been fucking's baby, and I will have no part in raising it. And if you want us to be together, if you truly see a future with me, you'll be in that abortion clinic as early as tomorrow morning." He continues his stubborn squabble.

"Calvin, just hear me out. We can't have children of our own... this is a blessing. We'll name it, we'll raise it, and we never have to tell it the truth if we never decide to. As far as anyone in the outside world is concerned, this will be your child. Plus, I think it will help our relationship, we'll learn to be fucking civilized and nicer to each other. This baby could fix us." I explain getting a little teary eyed my damn self.

"NAH, I'M GOOD! FUCK ALL OF THAT! I don't care what the outside world thinks or knows; I KNOW that the baby growing inside of you right now isn't mine! By the way, who the hell is the father anyways? Or do you not even know your damn self? You are just like everyone else, you're about to leave me because I'm nothing to you now, huh? I mean, I *am* a cripple that can't help out financially or even give you a damn baby, so why the fuck wouldn't you leave?" He cries.

"CALVIN, CALM DOWN BABY PLEASE! Listen… I could have left you ten years ago but I didn't, because I know if it wasn't for you I'd be dead right now. I owe you my life and I love you with all my heart." I meant everything I just said. I don't know where I'd be without Calvin. I don't care that he didn't have a dime or that he couldn't give me a baby, until recently I was prepared to live my entire life without children because I loved him *that* much. "And even if you didn't take that bullet for me, are you forgetting that I loved you way before I ever even met you?" I sigh then say, "Look, my baby's father is a millionaire TXA radio executive, okay? Hear me out. He's married! You hear me? Married! And it's to this big time newspaper chic I used to know, THERE IS NO WAY IN HELL HE WOULD LEAVE HER FOR ME EVEN IF I WANTED HIM TO."

'What's your point?" He barks.

"My point—*if you would have let me finish*— is that we'd be set for life! I wouldn't even have to put him on child support; I have visual proof of my night with him. I could blackmail him into giving us a monthly budget for me to keep my mouth shut. We'd be swimming in doe. And I'd put your name on the baby's birth certificate, and we would raise this beautiful blessing together… just me and you." I break down my plan to him.

"You are sick, you are really, really sick." Calvin mumbles as he limps off into the bathroom.

"Not sick, JUST EXTREMELY IN LOVE WITH YOU *and* excited about getting our family started!" I yell right back at him.

"Whatever." I hear him gabble. I then hear the bathtub filling up. Duggar must be getting ready to take one of his long soothing baths. He takes them a lot to help his joints and muscles; it also assists in subduing the reoccurring pain in his left leg. This gave me about an hour of alone time to watch and masturbate to the video of Jeremy and me. I have been watching it over and over again for the past four months since we made it. We truly created magic that night, every time I have a moment to myself in bed, I pull out my phone and reminisce.

Damn, I think as I touch myself. *We really got it in that night.* I really want to experience that kind of love making again. Sex with Duggar is great, don't get me wrong, but Jeremy had this aggression with him that made me fall in love with his dick. I knew that if I stuck with my original plan and immediately sent the video to Britney, Jeremy would hate me for life and I'd probably never get to fuck him again. So naturally, I decided months ago to hold off on the revenge plan until after I met with Jeremy at least one last time. Unfortunately, since that night, he's been dodging my calls and emails like the plague. Every time I call him he sends me straight to voicemail—and UGH! It's EXTREMELY frustrating, so much so that I can't even make myself cum to the video anymore; I'm just feenin' for the real thing. So I decide to make it my mission to have that dick one more time before I fuck him and his wife's marriage up forever.

~The Next Day~

I'm viewing the Jeremy and Jasmine homemade porn in my office when Dixie knocks on my door. I quickly shuffle and pull my skirt down and throw my cell phone into a drawer. Thankfully I had locked my office door otherwise she would've walked right in on me with one leg on my desk and two fingers vigorously rubbing my clit. I jolt up and unlock the door for her.

"Damn Jas, you barely come to the shop anymore and when you do, you spend all of your time cooped up here in your office, what's up?" She inquires.

"Nothing, I just have been having issues with Homeboy, that whole Miya thing has really been fucking with my head." I lie.

"Really? Damn. Well get over it." She snaps in an attempt to bring me back to reality.

"Wow, thanks *friend*." I respond sarcastically.

"You're lucky we're even still friends." She remarks, obviously joking. "I should have ended this friendship ten years ago when you moved in with the love of my life Homeboy MOTHERFUCKING Duggar. You know damn well he was and always will be my favorite rapper. I still, after all these years, can't believe you both are an actual *thing*." She laughs.

"Yea, sometimes I can't believe it either." I laugh along with her.

"In all seriousness Dy, you two are going to be fine. Calvin knows where his home is." She reassures me and calls me Dy which is short for Diamond *(my former dancer name)*.

"Yea girl, you're right." Little does she know that the real reasoning behind my dismay is the life growing inside of my stomach and the unrelenting yearning for Jeremy occurring in between my legs. My sudden change in character over the past four months had NOTHING to do with Duggar but EVERYTHING to do with Jeremy.

By the time noon rolls around, I decide I can no longer take the yearning so I grab my jacket from my office and storm out of the salon.

"Where are you going now?" I hear Dixie yell after me.

"Running a quick errand, I'll be right back." I lie again while continuing to make my way to my car. The truth is I am going to see Jeremy Rogers. Since the man won't answer any of my phone calls, I'm going straight to his place of business. I type TXA's address into my GPS and decide to take the hour long trip into Uptown Tooley.

"May I help you?' The receptionist politely questions me as I approach her desk.

"Actually yes, I'm looking to speak to Mr. Rogers. Is he available?" I ask just as politely.

"Jeremy? As in our CEO?" She responds with a smirk.

"Yas Jewemy, as-in-yow-CEO." I mock her, my politeness quickly disappearing.

"Well--" The young woman speedily gets on the phone and dials a number. "May I ask your name?" She remains professional but I can tell she's cursing me out in her mind.

"Tell him, Ivy is here to see him." I reply pompously.

"K." The once cheery receptionist retorts. "Hello Sir, there's a woman named Ivy here to see … yes… okay… yes Sir… I will. Okay. No problem, bye, bye. *click*" I see the smirk reappear on her face. "He's not in." She scoffs after hanging up the phone on whoever it was she got her marching orders from.

"Who's not in?" I'm becoming a little agitated.

"Mr. Rogers." She responds, this time with a full blown attitude.

"Oh really? It's 2PM on a Wednesday and your CEO who was just honored in TIME magazine for being one of the hardest working men of our generation isn't in his office? Pfft! Nice try."

"I mean—he was here, but he just stepped out for lunch." She sadly attempts to form an excuse out of thin air.

"Really? Lunch? Then why didn't you initially say that? LOOK bitch, do NOT bullshit me, I saw his car outside." It was the same Mercedes Benz he was driving the night we stayed at the Vacation Inn together and it was now parked directly outside in a reserved presidential parking space, so I basically caught the deceitful bitch in a lie.

"Ma'am, if you'd like me to leave a messa--"

"BITCH!" I get all in her face. "Call that man back RIGHT NOW and say if he doesn't agree to meet with me in the next five minutes his receptionist is going to be left in the same manner that I left the maid at the Ritz-Carlton in DC."

"Huh?" She probed with a look of confusion on her face.

"JUST DO IT!" I yell extremely loud which causes the on-duty security guard, who is seated not too far from us, to stand up.

"Everybody calm down, I'm here, I'm here." Jeremy appears from a winding hallway. "It's okay Gina, that's my cousin Ivy." He lies.

"Yea SIT DOWN, I'm FAMILY!" I snap at both the guard and the receptionist whose name is apparently Gina.

"Ivy," Jeremy laughs awkwardly, "now you settle down too… walk with me." Jeremy then leads me up the same winding hallway he appeared from. As soon as we are out of sight and ears reach he grabs my arm violently and pulls me into a random janitor's closet. "WHAT THE FUCK ARE YOU DOING HERE?" He maddeningly whispers.

"Came to see my long lost cousin, Jeremy." I laugh.

"CUT THAT SHIT OUT!" He scoffs tugging at my arm some more. "Are you fucking crazy? My wife could have been here and witnessed all that ruckus you just caused in my lobby."

"I'm sorry daddy; I just missed you so, so much." I coo while reaching for his groin. "You stopped returning my phone calls and just ignored me all together like I was nothing." Immediately we both jump at knocking coming from outside the door.

"What the hell?" I hear someone yelp.

"Shit." Jeremy mouths as he opens the closet door just enough to poke his head out of it. "Larry, hey."

"Mr. Rogers, I'm so sorry." The man says startled.

"No, Larry, don't be sorry. Look, I'm going to use your space for a few more minutes; I'll come and get you when I'm done in here okay? Just do me a favor and make sure no one else knocks on this door or tries to get in here again."

"Yes sir. I'm the only Janitor on duty today anyways." He jumps at his marching orders.

"Good, good." As soon as Jeremy is about to close the door again he calls for Larry his janitor one more time. "And Larry…"

"Yes sir."

"Do you mind not telling anyone I'm in here? If anyone asks this never happened."

"Uh yes sir, of course." Larry responds as if his job depended on it. Jeremy immediately closes the closet door.

"Look at you about to get me fucking caught up! What the fuck is wrong with you?" He barks at me.

"I miss my dick." I say flirtatiously.

"We agreed it was just a one-time fling." Jeremy says sternly while swatting away my advances.

"That was before I knew you could fuck like that. Damn daddy, you're all I think about." I immediately begin to strip all the way out of my clothing, when I'm done I stand directly in front of him in that tightly spaced closet, completely naked.

"You are crazy." Jeremy can't help but laugh at my antics as he shakes his head.

"…And you love it." I slyly reply as I begin kissing him on his neck.

"We can't do this." He says, this time with little to no resistance.

"Mmm baby, we can do whatever we want, you're the CEO." I begin sucking a little harder.

"Damn." He moans. I know now that he wants me just as bad as I want him. "Hold on, let me make sure this door is locked." Jeremy goes to the door again and once security is confirmed; he lays his blazer on the floor for us to use. "Okay we're going to do this quickly and this is the LAST TIME." He makes clear.

"Scouts honor." I lie as I help him take off his tie and unzip his pants. I move my hand over his manhood. Damn, he was already hard as a rock. I immediately kneeled over his jacket and began sucking his dick in the dark, musty Janitor's closet.

"DAMN." He moans. "Unfortunately I don't have time for foreplay I have a meeting with some big wigs in about an hour." He explains then lifts me to my feet. He takes out a condom from his wallet and hurriedly places it on his dick.

"We didn't use one the last time." I remind him.

"I know, and I couldn't sleep right for months. That was reckless, I'm sober right now; I was being drunk and irresponsible that night."

"Whatever." I say rolling my eyes. I decide to wait until after he fucks me good to tell him about our baby. Standing, Jeremy picks me up and rests me around his hips, pushing my back against a wall. I then wrap my legs around his waist as he begins to penetrate my pussy. It felt good but something was missing, it wasn't as angry or aggressive as the first time. Not to mention it was over before it began because he eventually came after only six or seven strokes. "Really?" I ask bluntly.

"I told you I have a meeting." He says gathering up all of his articles of clothing after he finishes and rids of the condom.

"One more round, please?" I beg while grabbing his arm.

"LOOK, WE SAID THAT WAS IT, SO NOW IT'S REALLY OVER! GO AWAY!" He says snapping at me.

"I'm pregnant." I blurt out hoping the information stabs him deeply in the heart for being so nasty to me.

"WHAT?" He says in a panic.

"I'M MOTHERFUCKING PREGNANT. Four months to the date to be exact." I badger.

"SHIT. I knew it." He barked. "I KNEW cumming inside of you would end bad… look…" Jeremy speedily takes out his wallet. "Here's about four hundred dollars, go get that taken care of." He demands.

"I'm keeping it." I inform him.

"Look, you're delusional. Call me later tonight and hopefully we can talk this out, but I'm busy as hell right now."

"Nothing to talk about, I'm having this baby, period. I drove damn near an hour to see you today; I'll just wait here for you until your very important meeting is over. I want my second round!" I contest.

"If you don't get the fuck out now, I'll have you dragged out!" Jeremy was done playing nice. Once we are both dressed he grabs me by the arm and drags me back into the lobby where the receptionist and security guard are.

"John, can you kindly escort Ms. Ivy off of the premises and please make sure she is never allowed inside of any of our TXA buildings again." John the security guard gets up and hastily walks towards me. At this point I become belligerent and start swinging my arms and legs.

"DO NOT FUCKING TOUCH ME!" I scream. Unfortunately, John the security guard is 6'4" and about three hundred, plus, pounds of pure muscle. He picks me up at the waist with one arm and carries me to the exit. I catch a glimpse of Gina-the-shady-receptionist's face and she's laughing hysterically.

"I WILL BEAT YOUR MOTHERFUCKING ASS!" I growl in her direction, wiping the stupid smirk right off of her face. "JEREMY YOU'RE GOING TO PAY FOR THIS SHIT, I SWEAR TO GOD YOU'RE GOING TO PAY FOR THIS!" I scream as John drops me off in the parking lot.

"Don't come back or I'll call the police." The guard sternly orders me while walking back inside the building.

"FUCK YOUUUU!" I scream after him. At this point I am crying hysterically. I did not expect Jeremy, *Mr. Nice Guy himself*, to treat me in this manner. It brings back memories of every single time a man has disrespected me in my lifetime and I become even more furious. I am COMPLETELY DONE keeping this baby a secret and protecting Jeremy. All I see is red as my entire body begins to tremble with anger. Time to take these skeletons out of the closet; release the big dogs; pull back the curtains, etc.… Jeremy will pay for this shit, way sooner than later.

Chapter 11: Weak Wives

~Present Day 2016~

I hate weak ass women! Women like Britney Rogers and my Aunt Leslie; they're the scums of the earth! They marry these venomous ass wolves in sheep's clothing and then once their spouses begin to reveal their true demented selves, who do those weak ass women blame? —none other than their husbands' victims. That's right; I was the fucking victim in BOTH cases when it came to my aunt and Britney. I wish I could just lock both women up in the same room and yell, *your fucking husbands put their penises inside of ME! I'M the fucking victim whether I provoked it or not!*

Hogan preyed on both Britney and I, but instead of joining forces with me to take him out in that law suit, she COMPLETELY shut me out... and *he* wasn't even her husband! Also my aunt was no different, she acted as though she was completely oblivious to my uncle's pedophilic behaviors and chose to turn a blind eye to the torment I underwent. That man raped me EVERY night for over a year and a half yet in her eyes, he could do absolutely no wrong...

~Flashback 1994~

"I'm pregnant." I couldn't believe I actually had the gall to finally let those two words escape from my mouth. At first I didn't even want to accept it myself... I would tell myself it was probably just a stomach ache or my period acting up, but after months of the same symptoms I finally took a pregnancy test and discovered the inevitable. My aunt was sitting across from me at our kitchen table and I remember the conversation as if it were yesterday.

"PREGNANT? What the hell is really going on here Jasmine?" She began to lecture me almost condescendingly. "I mean, your uncle and I have done nothing but try our best with you and now this?"

"It wasn't my fault." I murmured. I was sick of taking full responsibility for my uncle's behavior and I was done keeping him out of the lime light, but at the same time I still harbored the fear of going back into the foster care system. I remember thinking I had less than three years to go before I was officially an adult and I would finally be able to free myself from all the turmoil. I figured if

I just braced myself and endured my uncle's abuse for just a little while longer *(as opposed to going back into foster care and not knowing what to expect while in the custody of a completely new family)*, I'd be scotch free for the remainder of my life—obviously discovering I was pregnant was never factored into the plan.

    If only I was able to handle the termination of a pregnancy on my own, then I never would have come to my aunt for assistance and I could've avoided that ghastly conversation entirely. Unfortunately for me an abortion required money, and at fifteen years old I only had a good three dollars to my name. My aunt didn't work, but I knew she was the only one between us that could get any real money out of my uncle. I only really needed a hundred and seventy-five dollars and I figured they both owed me *AT LEAST* that.

    "Why the hell do you keep getting into these predicaments Jasmine? First you caught an STD last year and now you're pregnant? I understand it's rough on teenagers to have to grow up without their parents, BUT IT'S BEEN SEVEN YEARS! Stop acting out due to your losses and start being grateful for the resources you currently have!"

    "Don't talk about my parents." I grumbled. "Either loan me the money or don't, but leave my parents out of your mouth." I was fed up at this point.

    "Excuse me? You little ungrateful whore!" My Aunt Leslie snapped. "I HAVE DONE NOTHING BUT TAKE YOU IN AND LOVE YOU LIKE THE CHILD DENNIS AND I COULD NEVER HAVE! AND WHAT DO YOU DO? MAKE BAD DECISIONS AT EVERY TURN! The revealing clothes you wear… the dark cloud that always surrounds you… your bad grades… WHY ARE YOU LIKE THIS?" She continued in dismay.

    "You don't even know what the fuck I'm dealing with, so *please* spare me." I scoffed.

    "OH HELL NO!" Aunt Leslie said shocked, it was the first time I had ever cursed at her but I couldn't take any more of her idiotic lecture.

    "YOU DON'T KNOW SHIT ABOUT ME OR WHAT I'M GOING THROUGH!" I continued to snap. Immediately after I spoke I felt the back of my aunt's hand collide with the left side of my face.

"I refuse to raise a disrespectful whore!" She spat.

"I'M NOT A WHORE!" I stood up and grasped on to the pained side of my face. "I DON'T MESS AROUND WITH BOYS AUNTY AND THE ONLY MAN THAT'S EVER BEEN IN MY BED IS YOUR DAMN HUSBAND!" I finally let out.

"JESUS GIVE ME THE STRENGTH!" My aunt suddenly ran to her bedroom and in the blink of an eye she returned with one of her thickest belts. Before I even had the chance to flee, she immediately began nonsensically thrashing me. No other words were exchanged between us in that moment; just blow after blow to my back, my arms, and my legs... by the time she finally stopped beating me the skin over my entire body was either swollen or bleeding from gashes. Regardless of how much pain I was in I never gave her the satisfaction of seeing me cry; instead I retreated to my bedroom and silently sobbed myself to sleep while alone in there.

Later that same night after her temper had digressed and I was in my bed painfully attempting to get some rest, I heard my Aunt Leslie tiptoe into my bedroom. "You're a liar and a demon child but if you end up having that baby it will cost your uncle and I more than this procedure will. So after talking it out with him, we've decided to give you the damn money." She explained as if her statement had been rehearsed. I didn't even bother to turn around or acknowledge her; I kept my back to her and my tear-filled face to the wall. In that moment I had no idea if my aunt chose to ignore all the signs of abuse that went on under her roof in order to protect my uncle or if she actually thought he was innocent... either way I hated her for being a weak bitch. The dumb slut was so brainwashed that I felt sorrier for her than I did for myself. The truth is I was never as bad of a kid as she made me out to be and if it wasn't for her fucking husband I would have still been a virgin living out my childhood worry free. After she left my room I got up and retrieved the hundred and seventy-five dollars she left me on my dresser and used it later that week to terminate my pregnancy.

~Present Day 2016~

It should be extremely clear why I've never ever wanted to be someone's wife. Duggar has asked me to marry him a countless amount of times since we've been together and I've turned down every single one of his proposals. I refuse to be as pathetic as my aunt, she is no better than the dirt at the bottom of my shoe. She was so afraid to lose a man that she let him get away with everything under the sun. My birth mother was the only married woman that I have ever respected. From the little I remember about my parents' marriage, I know that my father adored and treated my mother like a queen. Of course in public she would give him the respect as head of household, but behind closed doors every decision was made with them being in agreeance. Men like my father are obviously a dying breed so to avoid being hitched to an asshole completely, I have just chosen to never submit to anyone at all!

Britney is also no exception. The bitch would probably blame me entirely for my current pregnancy when in reality, it takes two to tango. Yes, I chased after Jeremy initially in DC, but he still had a choice. And now this baby is here as a direct result of a jointly made bad decision.

I am in my car fuming from the embarrassment I have just endured at the TXA radio station. I've been calling Jeremy non-stop for the past hour and I've been driving aimlessly with a broken heart. Soon his phone stops ringing completely and just goes straight to voicemail. In order to clear my head, I pull over to the side of a random road where I notice the remains of a tossed newspaper sticking out from a grassy area. I can tell by the print it is a Tooley Times paper which furthermore infuriates me to the point of no return. That is the same paper Britney Rogers works as editor in chief for.

I immediately use my cell phone to google the general number to the Tooley branch's TXA headquarters building and dial the number.

"Thank you for calling TXA, Gina speaking, how may I transfer your call?" *FUCK*, I think to myself. Out of all people, Gina at the receptionist desk in Jeremy's building is the last person I want to speak to. Not knowing whether or not she remembers my voice, I act fast and attempt to disguise it.

"Ah yes, hello Gina, this is Mrs. Rogers." I take a deep breath in hopes that the imitation of my once best friend was adequate.

"Hello Mrs. Rogers." Gina responds, biting the bait.

"I'm sorry to bother you Gina, but I've been calling Jeremy's phone and it's been going straight to voicemail. Can you please transfer me to the phone in his office?" I continue.

"Yes ma'am." Gina responds cheerfully as she puts me on hold. I am so relieved that shit worked.

"Baby, I am so sorry, my phone died. Is everything okay? You don't normally call me around this time." Jeremy's voice finally comes bursting through the line.

"It's sad as fuck that I have to pretend to be your fucked up wife in order for you to have a civilized conversation with me, ASSHOLE!" I bark, wasting no time.

"I'm hanging up." Jeremy retorts.

"If you hang up the next number I dial will be Britney Rogers' at the Tooley Times paper." I threaten.

"Ok," I hear him take a deep breath, "you have my full attention."

"Oh I KNOW I do. YOU WANT TO HUMILIATE ME AND THROW ME OUT OF YOUR BUILDING WHEN I'M PREGNANT WITH YOUR BABY YOU PRICK? WELL YOU HAVE TO LEARN I AM NOT THE ONE TO BE FUCKED WITH!"

"Calm down, Jasmine, what are you going to do? Can we be civilized and talk all this through?" Jeremy asks, almost begging. I love hearing the vulnerability in his voice, he knows damn well he has messed up, he has messed up MAJORLY.

"Civil? Oh *no*, we are *WAY* past civil." I respond as I simultaneously shift my car out of park and begin driving again. This time I'm not steering aimlessly, instead I decide to purposely drive in the direction of the Tooley Times building. "I'M GOING TO YOUR WIFE'S JOB AND IM TELLING HER EVERYTHING. EVEN THE FACT THAT YOU GOT ME PREGNANT!" I scream into the phone.

"JASMINE, PLEASE STOP!" Jeremy panics.

"STOP? STOP WHAT? LOVING YOU? Because I can't just turn that switch on and off." I explain

"YOU DONT LOVE ME! HOW COULD YOU LOVE ME WHEN YOU'RE WITH HOMEBOY?" He asks exasperated.

"YES I DO, YES I DO, YES I DO!" I throw a slightly insane tantrum. "I just want us to all be one big happy family! You don't have to leave Britney and I won't leave Calvin, but Britney has to know TODAY in order for your disrespect towards me to stop!" I announce.

"YOU'RE CRAZY!" Jeremy repeats.

"You know I HATE when you call me crazy Jeremy, not to mention I'm almost at the Tooley Times. I'm actually looking forward to this reunion. I'm curious to see if Britney's body looks the same since having those two kids." I laugh making light of the very serious situation. I finally begin to turn into the paper's parking lot. "I'm here Jeremy!"

"DON'T DO ANYTHING CRAZY JASMINE!" Jeremy says in a threatening tone.

"All I want to do is introduce Britney to her step child." I cackle knowing his blood is boiling. "Like I said, we're all going to be one big happy messed up family after today." I turn my car off and I think Jeremy finally realizes how serious I am about everything.

"OKAY! STOP. OKAY. OKAY. You win! We'll figure something out together." He switches his tone out of desperation.

"Together?" I ask in order to reassure myself.

"Yes, together, just *please… Please* don't tell my wife PLEASE! If you love me like you say you do you won't tell my wife." He cries.

"Okay, Okay. It's no fun when you beg." I tease. "Meet me at the vacation Inn tonight and I won't go tell."

"I can't tonight Jasmine, I really can't tonight. I really did have back to back meetings today, there's a lot going on with the station." Jeremy spews out excuse after excuse.

"You know, I don't even have to get out of my car, I could just send her the video of us fucking that's in my phone RIGHT now!" I coldly reveal.

"PLEASE DON'T PLEASE JUST LISTEN GOD!" Jeremy exclaims. "I'll come out next weekend. It will be a slow work week for me and Britney and the kids will be on a school field trip in New York. I'll be alone and available to hear you out and we can work through all of this." He pleads sounding extremely genuine.

"Okay Jeremy, next weekend we're going to meet up and talk like we did the first time *and* we're going to be cordial. WHAT YOU'RE NOT GOING TO DO EVER AGAIN MR. ROGERS IS DISRESPECT ME LIKE YOU DID TODAY. DO I MAKE MYSELF CRYSTAL CLEAR?" I demand.

"Yes, Jasmine. I'll do whatever you say." After he says those last words I abruptly hang up on him, glare towards the building that holds my archenemy, and then solemnly drive away somewhat satisfied. Jeremy had better be present next weekend like he said he would, for his own good.

Chapter 12: Third Time's the Charm

~Present Day 2016~

I don't get home until around 11PM. It has truly been a long, emotional day. I've been driving for hours since I left the house to go to my shop at seven this morning. I went from work to the TXA office (which is about an hour away in Uptown Tooley), to the Tooley Times building (which is thirty minutes away from TXA), to now finally being back home (which took me hours because of traffic caused by an accident on the highway). I am EXHAUSTED, so imagine how annoying it was to turn the key to the front door and then immediately hear:

"WHERE THE HELL HAVE YOU BEEN?" Duggar is leaning on one crutch waiting by the front door.

"Who are you getting buck with? I was out doing things for the shop." I lie.

"Oh is that the code for fucking other men now? *Doing things for the shop*—my ass!" He scoffs.

"Look, I don't have to take any of this." I say as I shove my way past Duggar. Truth is, I am way too tired to deal with his bullshit right now. I've been in a car for hours, I've been up since 6AM, and I've been crying nonstop throughout it all… the *LAST* thing I want to do right now in this very moment is argue with his insecure ass.

"So you're just going to walk past me and ignore the problem? The house is a mess! There was barely any food for me to eat all day, and my laundry hasn't even been done!" He complains as I'm halfway up the steps.

"AND? You're a grown ass man! Do your own damn laundry! Clean up your own damn mess! And cook for your damn self!" I snap. I was reminded earlier today about how I never wanted to be a wife, but here I was stuck in this domestic situation that was extremely similar to the lifestyle I swore off. The thought of being submissive to a man pissed me off which is why I was giving Duggar such a hard time, even though had the roles been reversed and he stormed in at 11PM, I would have reacted in the same manner he did.

I bet if my mother had never been killed when I was eleven, I would have had completely different views on marriage. Unfortunately, my aunt was the only example of a wife I had been exposed to during some of the most important years of my development. Thanks to her, I've grown to detest everything 'tying the knot' stands for.

~Flashback 2005~

Years after I had been fired from Hogan & Wildes, LLP and was forced to go back to stripping at Sinsationals with Dixie, I remember having a deep conversation with her about our past. We couldn't come to grips about how we were in our mid-twenties but still leading the same pointless lifestyles. I was more depressed than she was because I felt I had experienced a taste of the good life by having worked for a nationally acclaimed law firm to then being fired for something out of my control and having to come right back to stripping. The entire ordeal was rather humbling and I would be lying if I said I wasn't extremely depressed in the beginning of that year.

Of course this particular conversation had occurred about six months before I met Duggar for the second time since being gang banged by him and his crew, and it would be a good nine months before I was lucky enough to be contacted by a lawyer about a class action lawsuit against Hogan's firm, so I really had no way of knowing that there would actually be much more to my life.

Sinsationals had just closed for the night and we both were taking our time talking in the locker room. Dixie was a great confidant back then; of course I never shared with her about killing my uncle and testifying against Gary "Killa" Lewis over eight years earlier, but we always delved deep about our childhoods. In that particular conversation she made a good point out of desperation; what if my birth parents or even the state had left some money behind for me for when I turned eighteen? I didn't think that was a farfetched idea being as though most responsible parents did that for their children. Also, before my parents died there was a lot of talk about us moving from Chicago to somewhere safer and I remembered them being fairly close to their financial goal, whatever that figure might have been. So I agreed with Dixie when she said there must be some money somewhere left for me. The very next day after our conversation I decided to do the unthinkable which was call my Aunt Leslie and ask. I figured if anyone would know if I was owed any money from the government or my parents, Aunt Leslie would know.

Dixie and I were living in extremely poor conditions. We had been stripping for little to no money because I remember times were rough that particular month. Even though our rent was really cheap thanks to section eight housing, we barely had enough food to eat on a day to day basis so my desperation led me to do what I told myself I'd never do once I left Chicago—contact my aunt.

"Hello?" I remember hearing her very familiar voice pick up on the other end of the phone. I called her from a payphone because I recall never wanting her to be able to contact me after I got the information I needed.

"Hello Aunt Leslie, it's me... Jasmine." I replied timidly. I was a little taken aback that I was a twenty-six-year-old grown woman but I still feared my aunt's authority, I couldn't believe I trembled at her voice even after all those years apart.

"JASMINE? Lord... where the hell have you been? I was worried sick! I thought the gang you were living with had come and kidnapped you after you testified against Killa."

"No aunty, I just left, there was nothing left for me in Chicago." I admitted.

"You left me too Jasmine, and it's been rough over here without you or Uncle Dennis. I might have to sell the house; I've really been going through a lot." She complained. I remember thinking *she hasn't changed*. I, her young niece, have been away from my aunt for over eight years after I ran away in the middle of the night at age seventeen and the first thing she talks about are *her* troubles? What about mine? Didn't she want to know more about how I was or who I'd been staying with? The conversation just reminded me more about why I hated her, but for the sake of finding out information, I bit my tongue.

"Sorry to hear all of that, life has been tough over here on this end too." I offered up.

"Nobody made you leave Jasmine; we could have got through everything together." She nagged.

"Yea." I said knowing damn well if I would have stayed she would've tortured me or kept blaming me for her husband's death (since according to her, I was the one who brought that boy Killa into their lives). She still had no idea I was the one who actually killed my uncle, and more importantly, neither did the police.

"So you coming back home? Maybe we could start a new life together… If we both get a job, we can get me out of debt and keep the house." She explained excitedly.

"I just don't think Chicago is for me, aunty." I responded honestly.

"Well maybe then I can move to wherever you are?" She blurted out. "I could just foreclose and move in with you, where do you live?" She eagerly invited herself into my life.

"Aunty, I don't think that's a good idea either, I don't live alone right now." I informed her, and honestly even if I was a billionaire at the time living in my own mansion instead of living in Dumois with Dixie, I STILL wouldn't let my aunt stay with me.

"Well then, why'd you call?" She asked bluntly, turning into the smart-mouthed bitch I remembered.

"I just had a question. Like you said, times have been hard… and… and… well…"

"Just spit it out." She growled.

"And I just wanted to ask if my parents or the government or even Uncle Dennis left me any money." I finally let out. Yes, I asked about Uncle Dennis' money as well because after all the hell he put me through, I was OWED at least something. I heard my aunt laughing hysterically before she responded.

"Like a trust fund?" She continued to bawl on the other end of the phone. "You think you're a trust fund baby or something?"

"No, I just thought my parents had a little bit of money they were putting away before they died for us to move out of Chicago. I don't care if the amount is less than a thousand dollars, anything right now would help me out." I pleaded.

"That's why you called, huh?" She remarked.

"Yes… but forget it." I was frustrated with how she was treating the situation and at my wits end. For all I cared, she could keep her attitude as well as any knowledge of any funds from my parents.

"Quit being a big baby, yes you have a little bit of money. I've been holding it for you here until you tuurned eighteen." She finally disclosed.

"From my parents?" I asked hoping that was the case. That would solidify their awesomeness.

"Yea, a little from your parents, a little from your uncle and a little from me. We've always wanted what was best for you, Jasmine." She explained. I suddenly took back every bad thing I had ever said about the old hag, the fact that she was in possession of some money for me and didn't use it on her own expenses, but kept it in case I ever contacted her again, said she really did care about me deep down.

"Can you please wire me some of the money aunty?" I begged.

"It's yours, Jasmine... BUT... you have to come get it. I saved it for you, the least you can do is come visit me one more time before you go back to your regularly secluded life." She negotiated.

"Okay." I agreed. I figured the least I could do was give her one last face to face meeting. The next day one of the other dancers loaned me the sixty dollars I would need to take buses to and from Chicago.

I arrived at my aunt's doorstep in Chicago three days after our initial phone conversation. I remember having chills go up and down my spine as my mind flooded with memories, both good and EXTREMELY bad, of that house.

"Jasmine!" My aunt swooped down the steps and embraced me before I even had the chance to knock on her door.

"Hey aunty!" I responded faking my enthusiasm. She looked terrible, she never did drugs when I was younger but she must have started to dabble in them after the death of her husband because the body weight she once held had dropped immensely. Her face looked skinny in a *crack addict* type of way not an *ooh girl you've been working out* fashion.

"Come... come inside!" She joyously pulled me by my sleeve into the morbid house. The home's condition was extremely poor compared to how I remembered it. It looked like one of those houses on the show Hoarders. I guess with my uncle not being around to strong hand her into cleaning up, and even her not having me around to make do her chores, she let the whole place go to shreds. "Wait right here! I'll be right back! Going to get your check!" She left me in the living room as she pranced upstairs.

Maybe a teenage me would have bought into her awkward behavior, but at that point I had been through entirely too much for her to think I was naïve enough to not question her rather strange behavior. So being the street-smart girl that I am, moments later I followed her to her bedroom, where her door was cracked and I noticed she was sitting on her bed, whispering on the phone.

"Yes she's here… Killa she's right here in my living room. I told you I'd call as soon as I got her here. I did good right? …She has no idea… Two hours? …Okay I'll try my best to stall her." I heard her whisper. From what I gathered by her conversation, my dumb ass aunt was on the phone with Killa letting him know I was in her house. This whole meeting was a trap and I had approximately two hours before I was shark food.

As soon as my aunt hung up the phone I ran to her and strangled her old ass with my bare hands. I had a pistol on me for protection because I knew I was coming into old territory where many people were out to get me; Killa, Killa's gang, other people I had robbed when I was with Killa. I knew I couldn't just show up in Chicago without a weapon, but I never thought in a million years my aunt would be the one I'd think about using it on.

"WHAT THE FUCK WAS THAT ALL ABOUT?" I scream as I use my entire strength to surround her fat neck with my fingers.

"I… I can't breathe… please…" She struggled to let out. That's when I let go of her neck and pushed her off of the bed on to her knees. I pulled out the gun I had hidden on my body, cocked it, and then aimed it directly at her forehead. "Jasmine, what's all this? What's gotten into you?"

"Don't act dumb you stupid bitch, you know EXACTLY why I have this gun aimed at your dome." I spew venomously. "Want to explain what the hell that little conversation was about?"

"I… I…" My aunt began to stutter, I guess she hadn't anticipated on my following her up the steps to her bedroom and listening in on her conversation. I was a fairly respectful child, even when I moved back in with my aunt after Killa was arrested, so this aggressive personality I had acquired later on in my life was new to her.

"Stop stuttering bitch, I'm not stupid! You just got off the phone with Killa to warn him about where the hell I was, so now I need to get the hell out of town he shows up and kills me. So Leslie, what I need you to do at this very moment is get me the money you promised me QUICK so I can start making my way out of town." I commanded.

"Baby I'm sorry, I'm so, so sorry… Killa put me up to this! Ever since he got out of jail on parole he's been breathing down my neck trying to find you." She cried.

"Okay, so the fuck what? You couldn't tell him you had no idea where I was?"

"I've been doing that for the past eight years but he's not stupid, Jasmine. He even has a reward out for your head!" She revealed. That's when I finally cocked my gun.

"So that's why you would turn against your own family? – For the reward money?" I was extremely livid at this point. I knew my aunt was lowly but that situation was an all-time low for her.

"No baby, never… he just knew you were coming… I couldn't lie to Gary…" She pleaded.

"FUCK ALL THAT BULLSHIT! You picked another fucking man over me for the second time in your life." I barked.

"What are you talking about?" She asked, confused.

"Uncle Dennis! You put that pig over me… Do you even know what the fuck he used to do to me? You fucking husband raped me!" I yelled. I've told my aunt the truth on so many occasions but all my life she'd accuse me of lying or beat me before I could tell my complete story… but not this time. This time I had the upper hand, and it felt GREAT! "He came in to my room after my fourteenth birthday and for almost two years he fucking raped me every night! Remember the Chlamydia and the baby? –That was all your sick ass husband's doing! I tried to tell you, I tried to tell you time and time again, but aunty YOU'D BEAT ME!" I cried maniacally. My aunt just kneeled there silent; she had nothing to say to me which was a first for her. I was convinced this bitch had no heart. "SO YOU'RE NOT GOING TO SAY ANYTHING?"

"You… you ruined my marriage." I finally heard her let out.

"What?" I couldn't believe what I had just heard.

"I thought because I couldn't have kids, adopting you would help our marriage out, but when you got older… all his attention went towards you and off of me. You hurt us instead of helped us." She admitted.

"HE RAPED ME, I NEVER ASKED FOR ANY OF THAT, I CAME TO YOU FOR HELP AND ALL YOU DID WAS BEAT ME!" I cried. "YOU KNEW THIS WHOLE TIME I WAS TELLING THE TRUTH? DID YOU KNOW WHAT HE DID TO ME ALMOST EVERY NIGHT UNDER THIS ROOF! YOU WERE SUPPOSED TO PROTECT ME! YOU NEVER LOVED ME!" I continued to wail.

"YOU WEREN'T MINE!" She spat back in my face. The angry aunt I was used to know had resurfaced and the 'cowardly old woman front' she had put on for me since I arrived disintegrated faster than sugar in water. "You were just dropped in my lap and you ruined my family dynamic. He was so busy fucking you he didn't have sex with me. At first I thought you were our salvation but you turned into my worst nightmare… I hated having you around."

"I can't believe all these years, you've known." I repeated her in disbelief. I fell to the floor in emotional shock and pain. I had no idea a human being could be so cruel. She was worse than my uncle. She had no soul. I got up to leave, by this time twenty minutes had passed and I didn't want to be there when Killa arrived.

"Your vendetta should be with yourself, you know. You were always wearing tight jeans and frolicking around in the house." She unexpectedly added.

"Oh my fucking GOD, I was a child! Are you REALLY blaming ME for what your sick husband did to me?" I stopped in my tracks to respond.

"YES! YOU ARE A WHORE!" She blurted out. That's when I lost complete control of my emotions. My sadness had turned into pure hatred and anger. I aim my gun again, this time at her temple, before she could even say her next statement or protest I pulled the trigger and once I knew she was dead, I ran. My Aunt Leslie was the third person I've ever killed—and I don't regret it.

Chapter 13: Pure Luck

~Flashback 2005~

Two months had passed since I killed my aunt and I was back in Dumois living my life under the radar. I had been working like a horse, not only dancing but picking up day time shifts at a Burger Royale to make ends meet. With the extra income I was able to pay the girl that loaned me the sixty dollars for my trip back, as well as catch Dixie and I up on our bills. Dixie asked why I didn't return with that lump sum my aunt had given me and I lied and told her some guys robbed me at a pit stop and I never made it all the way to Chicago and she believed me. I told her I thought my aunt had set me up so I didn't plan on ever returning.

One morning when I was working drive-thru at the Burger Royale, my shift manager approached me and sternly told me to follow him to the back room. He told me the FBI was on the phone and specifically asked for me. My heart stopped, I had a feeling my murderous rampage had come back to haunt me. I just knew that they had finally discovered that I was responsible for both the deaths of my Uncle Dennis and Aunt Leslie. Before I got to the back room I contemplated running away, not just from the Burger Royale restaurant but leaving Missouri entirely. Being a fugitive or going to jail, those were basically my only two options and I had to pick one—quickly. When my manager opened the door to the back room, I took a deep breath and turned to run but another fellow employee was right behind me, blocking my path. Startled, I immediately changed my mind and shook off any thoughts of running away, my manager never even noticed my brief hesitation. I took that moment as a sign for me to just go ahead and deal with the inevitable as I walked into the tiny room and took the phone from my manager's hand.

"I don't know what it's about, but if you're in any kind of legal trouble this will be your last day here." He barked before releasing the hold button and leaving me alone in the back room.

"Jasmine speaking." I say into the phone.

"Hello Jasmine, this is Detective McNeal. I am one of the officers that worked on your uncle's case back in the late nineties... do you remember me?" Chills ran up and down my spine.

"Yes." My response barely escaping my lips.

"Okay good, how have you been?" He asked in a failed attempt at alleviating some of the tension. I remember wishing he would just get to the point and finally say something along the lines of: we have the restaurant surrounded and I want you to come out with your hands up—but he doesn't, so I continue to go along with the small talk.

"I've—I've been good." I nervously let out.

"Good. Anyways, you are very hard to find. We had to pull your social in order to find you and the only two hits available were a job you had in Tooley in 2000 at Hogan & Wildes, LLP and this one." He chuckled, still trying his best to make light of a morbid conversation.

"Oh…" I responded not knowing why he was being so cheerful.

"Anyways, I know you probably haven't gotten over the death of your uncle but I'm sad to inform you that your aunt was killed two months ago as well." He finally discloses the reason for his call.

"OH MY GOD!" I gasped. I figured I'd play along since he hadn't accused me of anything yet.

"I know, I know, she was the only family you had left. I'm just glad you weren't harmed. We have reasons to believe Killa killed her." WHAT? My mind almost exploded… HOW THE HELL DO THEY THINK KILLA KILLED MY AUNT? In an attempt to prevent myself from jumping up and down for joy and busting out in laughter right there on the phone in the detective's ear, I bite my lip. "You see," Detective McNeal continued. "I have been trying to contact you for two months now to possibly put you on witness protection. As soon as Gary was released on parole your aunt came up dead, not to mention we have on record that his was the last phone number she contacted before she was gruesomely shot in the head. We found her body in her bedroom; Gary is not playing Ms. Hall. I think he is coming for you next. He spent the last eight years in prison blaming you for the murder of your uncle; it wasn't until he finally admitted his wrong doings that he became eligible for parole. Now if you don't mind me asking, what made you move to Dumois?"

"I—I was scared for my life. I wanted to get out of Chicago, you know? I've witnessed way too many deaths there, from my parents to my uncle… and now even my aunt! I just couldn't take the atmosphere." I lied. Even though my statement was somewhat true, that was only partially why I fled. Majority of why I left my aunt's house in the middle of the night when I was only seventeen years old to come to Dumois (a city I was barely familiar with), was because it was a quiet town out of the radar where I knew Killa or his boys would never find me.

"Completely understandable, since you're already basically in hiding there's no need to put you in witness protection. Just do yourself a favor and stay in that town and lay low, do NOT, I repeat DO NOT come back here to Chicago! Gary has missed all of his meetings with his parole officers and is now an escaped felon. If you hear anything from him on your end do not hesitate to contact me, but Jasmine, until he is caught STAY AWAY! I cannot stress that enough!" He sternly advised me. What he didn't know was he damn sure didn't have to tell me twice. There was nothing about Chicago I would EVER miss… except the early moments of life that I shared with my parents of course.

~Flashback 1987~

Is it odd that my most vivid memory of my parents wasn't something phenomenal but rather just a regular day? Nonetheless, I remember it as if it were yesterday:

I was eight years old and my mother, Eva, had just picked me up from school and I tagged along as she went to the grocery store.

"Wow, the price of potatoes has surely gone up." I remember her making small talk with the cashier who she knew by name. My mother was a people person, every memory I have with her talking to people, the other person is always smiling. Even though I was young when she passed away and didn't delve into grown-up affairs, I just know in my hearts of hearts that she had absolutely no enemies. I recall that on that particular day my mother was one item over her budget and the cashier actually paid the remainder balance for her. (My mother was really thankful and weeks later ended up repaying the cashier with interest for their generosity). Anyways, after that particular grocery run and other errands, we went home.

"One day you're going to have a family of your own Jasmine and hopefully you'll never have to struggle to make ends meet—if you listen to your father and I you won't ever have to." I remember my mother saying as I followed her to the back yard with four potatoes in her hand. "Just in case you are ever in a situation like I was in today, I'm going to teach you how to plant your own crops."

"Yes ma'am." I answered her and then watched as she planted the potatoes in the ground and other seeds in her garden for the next hour. My mother had a beautiful garden, tomatoes, potatoes, peanuts, and more were at her finger tips. We barely went to the grocery store, but that day we were low on produce, so she went.

By the time my father got off work at about 7PM my mother had picked me up from school, ran errands, planted crops, did my laundry, and cooked the three of us an amazing meal. She did all that after working her own 7AM-3PM job at a thrift store. She was an extremely hard worker so it was refreshing when my father, Cyrus, came through the door with flowers he had hand-picked on his way back from work and a love note he had handwritten while at work. He was a janitor of a really bad public school in Chicago, so the fact that his weary days cleaning up after misguided children didn't stunt his romantic side was beautiful.

They deserved each other, my parents. That day after he handed my mother her flowers she ran and jumped into his arms as if he had gotten her a diamond necklace. During their embrace, an eight-year-old-me would make a disgusted face because back then I didn't understand love. My parents would look over at me and laugh and then chase me around trying to catch me. Once they did they both showered me with hugs and kisses and fell to the ground laughing and being joyous.

That was one of the best days of my life. Despite all the things we lacked financially, my parents made it all up in love. We would all eventually sit around a table, pray, and then eat the delicious food my mother prepared from literally SCRAPS. She turned the little we had in the house to eat into a gourmet three course meal, my father called my mother a magician. After dinner my father washed all the dishes and made sure I took a bath and got ready for bed. He gave my mother a foot-massage while I was getting ready and once I was in my bed they both came and read to me for about thirty minutes. And I don't mean just an average reading; they went all out, jumping on my bed, acting out each character in my book… I mean, we didn't have a television growing up but we didn't need one. My parents were entertaining enough!

    Anyways, that's one of the days I spent with my parents that I remember vividly to this day. I will always love and miss them, they truly were amazing people. I probably would have turned out extremely different had they never been gunned down three blocks from our home almost four years later. Even though they were only in my life for a short period of time, it was pure luck that I ever had those two as parents at all.

Chapter 14: Kill or Be Killed

~Present Day 2016~

  It's been two days after the whole TXA ordeal with Jeremy and I am exhausted. I have just pulled into my driveway and I want nothing more than to go straight to sleep. I left work early because I've been having intense migraines, probably from all the screaming and yelling I did with Jeremy on the phone. I know Dixie is probably fed up with all my bullshit; leaving work early, calling in sick, taking off for doctor visits… I'm just thankful that I'M the owner and she's MY employee otherwise she'd probably fire me.

  I walk into the house after checking the mailbox and the first thing I hear is moaning. When I turn into the living room I see the most heart wrenching display; Calvin is lying on our couch and a woman I don't know is on top of him, riding his brains out.

  "WHAT THE FUCK IS GOING ON?" I scream at the top of my lungs. Embarrassed, they both scurry to grab their clothing.

  "You're home early." Duggar awkwardly responds as if there was nothing else that needed to be addressed.

  "WHO THE HELL IS THIS?" I bark. I am so close to ripping off both of their heads.

  "I'm Miya." The masculine looking woman responds.

  "BITCH! DO NOT ADDRESS ME IN MY OWN HOUSE! Matter of fact, GET THE HELL OUT BEFORE I CATCH MY FIRST CASE! AND IF I EVER SEE YOU IN THIS DAMN HOUSE AGAIN I'LL KILL YOU!" I threaten her. She jumps back because I have that *I'm not playing* look written all over my face.

  "I'll be in the car." She says meekly to Duggar who is struggling with his belt.

  "Man, if you don't GET THE HELL OUT!" I launch in her direction. Miya hurriedly grabs the rest of her things and sprints towards the door before she even has the chance to finish buttoning up her blouse.

  "I finally meet the extraordinary Miya." I mock Duggar after she's finally out of the house. "THAT'S WHO YOU'RE LETTING DISRESPECT ME?" I laugh. Miya wasn't competition to me at all, she had manly features, she was awkwardly tall but freakishly skinny and her weave looked a mess. Also she looked older than

Duggar with lots of plastic surgery done to her face, what the hell could he possibly be getting from her that he wasn't getting from me?

"I don't want to do this." Duggar responds, a little ashamed.

"Oh, we're going to do this, baby, BETTER BELIEVE THIS WILL BE DONE!" I snarl.

"Jasmine, calm down, that pregnancy got you all discombobulated because I don't know what the HELL makes you think you can talk to me the way you've been talking to me." Calvin says, finally regaining his balls.

"*I'M* DISRESPECTING *YOU*? I just came home to MY house and you have this manly looking bitch in here riding you on MY couch, are you out of your GOT-DAMNED mind?" I ask livid.

"See there you go again with that *my* house shit. It's always *my, my, my,* with you. What about MY fucking leg, huh? Or did we forget about that? WHAT ABOUT *MY* FUCKING OPINION ON YOU HAVING THAT BASTARD CHILD OF YOURS? FUCK ALL THAT *MY, MY, MY,* SHIT!" He spat.

"So what now—you want to leave me for that manly looking ape outside?" I inquire because I see Duggar putting on his shoes and jacket. "You're really about to leave with her?" I repeat in disbelief.

"Man, you're so full of shit. How can you stand here pregnant with another man's baby and question what the hell I'm about to do with my life? The way I see it, if you have this baby, I'm gone." He says questioning my hypocrisy and providing me with an ultimatum.

"I'm sorry Calvin, I really am. I know you don't want me to have this baby, but I can't give it up." I explain.

"Then I'm gone." He responds coldly.

"WHAT THE HELL DOES SHE DO FOR YOU THAT I DON'T?" I screech when I realize he isn't playing and is about to leave me for that ugly, lanky girl with the bad weave.

"She listens, cleans up, cooks every night, and doesn't make me feel like less of a man because I'm crippled or jobless. Jasmine, you've nagged me and disrespected me for the past ten years, yes you do a lot for me but you always hold it over my head like I haven't done shit for you. You act like I'm no good; you even had the audacity to get knocked up by another man! –And then expect me to want you to keep it! I can NOT stress it enough how disrespectful that shit is, whether or not we have an open relationship. So why you're tripping about me leaving right now is beside me!" He argues.

"FINE!" I snap. "YOU GET THE HELL OUT OF MY HOUSE TOO! DON'T COME BACK WHEN YOU'RE SICK OF LOOKING AT THAT UGLY BITCH!" I continue screaming as I trail him into the yard. That's when I notice Miya's ugly ass peering from inside of her beat up Honda Civic parked across the street. "I DID EVERYTHING FOR YOU AND YOU HAD THAT BROKE ASS UGLY ASS HOE IN MY HOUSE? ENJOY EACH OTHER! Y'ALL BOTH BROKE AND BUSTED!" Before I could let out another word, Miya speeds off with Duggar riding shotgun, giving me the finger in the process. *Fuck both of them*, I think to myself as I go back inside the house.

I've had an extremely long week. First my dealings with Jeremy and now my number one, Calvin, is acting up as well. How did I get here, in this dark emotional state? When I got back in the house from yelling at Miya and Calvin, I made myself some food and went straight to bed. That was at around 3PM and it's now one in the morning. I decide to turn off the television and other distractions and actually get some rest. Who knows, I might call out of work tomorrow and let Dixie handle the workload because I'm not emotionally sound. As soon as I begin to shut my eyes to get some sleep my phone rings.

"Hello?" I answer a bit hopeful that it's Duggar calling me back to reconcile our differences and come home.

"…." All I hear on the other end of the phone is heavy breathing.

"Hello?" I repeat, "Duggar?"

"…" Again silence.

"Look, I feel bad too, just come home baby." I plead with who I think is Calvin. It has to be him because no one else would have the gall to call my home at 2AM. All the sudden I hear some familiar laughter but I can't quite grasp who it is, the only thing I know is it's not Duggar. "Hey… who the hell is this? It's 2AM and I'm not here for the games!" I snap at the unidentified prank caller.

"Jasmine, lighten up." The person finally speaks. Again, the voice is familiar but I can't put a name to it.

"Who is this?" I ask one more time.

"That's not important. What's important is, I have a tombstone with your name on it." And just like that they hang up.

"Holy fuck", I say to myself, *"Killa."* I IMMEDIATELY spring out of bed and begin to pack a bag, I don't know where I'm going to go but I sure as hell can't stay here. If that man knows my phone number, he knows my address. I begin to tremble at the thought of it already being too late and expect him to be right outside of my front door. Hopefully he is still in Chicago... but I'd rather be safe than sorry. I maniacally continue to shove lots of clothes and shoes in the bag. *Hurry Jasmine, HURRY!* I think to myself. The last thing I pack is my hand gun, the same one I used to kill my Aunt Leslie. I've been keeping it hidden in a loose floorboard in my bathroom; Duggar doesn't even know it exists. He would probably be pissed if he knew I kept a gun being as though a gun is the reason he's crippled now, but I honestly had no choice.

I run to my car and take about three minutes to steady my trembling hands in order to put my key into the ignition. Finally, the car starts and I race off to nowhere. There was no way in hell I was going to stay anywhere near my house assuming Killa knew of my whereabouts. I also drove in and out of alleyways to make sure no one was tailing me.

*RING, RING! * my cell phone goes off scaring me half to death. "Hello?" I answer using my car's Bluetooth speaker.

"JASMINE, OH MY GOD WHERE ARE YOU?"

"Dixie?" I ask for a confirmation, somewhat relieved it isn't Killa calling my cell phone. That would have been too much for me.

"JASMINE, THE SHOP IS ON FIRE!" She continues in a panicked tone.

"WHAT?" I ask in disbelief.

"SOMEONE SET THE SHOP ON FIRE, OH GOD! THE FIRE DEPARTMENT CALLED ME FROM HOME ABOUT FIVE MINUTES AGO, I'M ON MY WAY THERE NOW!" She shrieks. Even though I am the owner, I had the fire department and police station list Dixie as the emergency contact since she spends the most time at the salon.

"OH MY GOD!" I reply, this just is not my day. First a threat from a man I've been hiding from for the past nineteen years, and now my shop is on fire! "I AM ON MY WAY!" I tell Dixie. As soon as I hang up, that's when I put two and two together. Killa might be setting me up, he's not one to call and threaten, he's more like the type to just aim and shoot to kill. I doubt he actually had my home address; he must've gotten my home number from a listing. I'm a thousand percent sure he is behind the burning of my salon. He probably did it to lure me out to the scene this late at night. I knew what kind of cold blooded killer Gary "Killa" Lewis was and I wasn't going to take any chances. Even if police and firemen surrounded the scene, he's the type that would shoot me in broad daylight and then put a bullet through his own skull. I am going to go with my gut, play it safe and stay away from all things that reek of Killa. I decide to call Dixie back immediately.

"Listen girl, the same kinds of people involved in paralyzing Duggar are back and after me. I think they might be responsible for burning the salon down. I'm going to lay low for now; I'm scared to even go to the police because that's what they probably expect me to do. Please, please, please, just handle what you can on your own." I beg her hoping she understands.

"Oh my God Dy, that's fine… just please stay safe. I'm here now and it's literally burned to the ground. I don't know if there's any coming back from this." She cries. Dixie loved that shop just as much as I did. It was a way for her to get out of the hood. With her salary as shop manager she was able to move out of low income housing and into a home of her own. That shop has put money in the pockets of a lot of former Sinsationals dancers—and it's all gone now.

"Thank you." I express to her before hanging up. My emotions are in a whirlwind. I don't know if I'm scared, angry, heartbroken, or suffering from morning sickness, but I need help so I do the unthinkable and call Jeremy. I know it's late but he is the only one I can think of calling. Duggar had left his cell phone behind when he left with Miya, I'm pretty sure it was his way of saying 'KEEP YOUR HOUSE AND THE PHONE YOU BOUGHT ME'—so I honestly knew of no one else to call. Finally, after sending me to voicemail a million times, Jeremy answers his phone.

"Hello?" He whispers, "What are you doing calling me at two thirty in the morning?"

"I'm—I'm sorry…"

"Damn right you're sorry! My wife was lying right beside me; I had to run to the bathroom to answer this call." He angrily informed me.

"I'm sorry, I need help. Your baby and I are in extreme danger. PLEASE, I could be dead by tomorrow. I don't have the money to get a room for a long stay, my shop just burned down; I don't have anywhere to go…please." I beg.

"Okay… okay… calm down." I think Jeremy can sense the sincerity in my voice because he immediately changes his tone. "Go to the vacation Inn, I'll book you a room for two weeks under my name. I'll also still come see you this weekend as planned, but after Saturday I want absolutely nothing to do with you, you hear me? I am doing my part, but on Saturday you have to stop putting my relationship in danger." He adds sternly.

"Okay." I respond solemnly. I really had no choice, he was practically saving my life at the moment, I wasn't going to argue. Jeremy immediately hangs up. He must love me if he's willing to get this room; if he really wanted nothing to do with me he would have just ignored me. There HAS to be something there, especially now that Duggar and I were practically over. I checked into the room Jeremy booked and I immediately got under the covers fully clothed. I am hoping as soon as I shut my eyes to sleep, I'll wake up and all this entire mess will be a dream. Jeremy, Killa, Duggar, the shop on fire, etc.… It can't all be real. If only that was the case, unfortunately it isn't, especially the Killa part. He is after me and the only way I can live my life without fearing him is if I find him before he finds me and kill him. Kill Killa or be killed? –*THAT* is the question.

Chapter 15: Us against the World

~Present Day 2016~

Sick of Vacation Inn breakfasts, I decide to scrap up all the loose change and the dollar bills I have at the bottom of my purse and make my way across the street to the Morehouse Coffee Shop. It's been three days since I received that unnerving phone call from Killa and thanks to Jeremy Rogers paying for my hotel costs, I've been able to stay low-key and avoid possible discovery. It's Saturday morning, the day Jeremy promised to come see me to talk about our differences, but I have yet to hear from him.

"I'll just have bacon and cheese on a croissant and some orange juice." I tell the barista. (Even though I am at Tooley's finest coffee shop I don't include a cup of joe in my order because remember, I only drink coffee at night especially since I add a little *kick* to it).

"Will that complete your order?" The handsome employee asks with a huge smile.

"Yes." I respond. I'm used to getting attention from men. Sometimes I recognize some as former patrons of Sinsationals who remember me from my dancing days. This particular man didn't look familiar to me at all though. Once my food is prepared, I take it to a table and sit down. That's when I see the same barista leave his post at the register and walk towards me with a broom. He begins sweeping under the unoccupied tables around me. *Okay, what's this guy's deal?* I think to myself. "Do I know you?" I bluntly confront the employee when I catch him glaring in my direction.

"Yes… well… no. I've just seen you here plenty of times. You actually used to come in almost like every night but you haven't been here in a while." He reveals.

"Oh… so you're stalking me?" I ask, getting straight to the point. I think my stripper days have hardened the way I interact with men. I like to say that there's nothing soft about me but my breasts, thighs, ass, and skin… and hair and hands… but you get the point—I don't take any shit.

"No, no." The barista laughs. "Like I said, I just notice whenever you're here."

"Oh so you're saying I'm noticeable?" I flirt back.

"Very. You're an extremely beautiful woman." He says while blushing a little bit.

"Aww, thank you. You're not so bad yourself." I smile. I wasn't lying either, I could tell behind his uniform and apron there was a good looking guy underneath. He appeared to have a great body, great hair, and a nice smile. His skin was dark and beautiful, which is normally my preference with an exception of Duggar who is farer than me. Killa and most other men of my past have been dark-skinned. His only downfall is that he's around my age working as a barista, as shallow as it sounds, I only like dealing with accomplished men. Again—I made another exception for Duggar because he saved my life and even though he doesn't have money now, he has already created a lifelong legacy for himself.

"So, does that mean I can get your number?" He boldly comes out and asks.

"Listen, you're a great looking guy… but…"

"But what?" He interjects, "What this uniform? I know what it looks like, but I'm not just a barista. Plus, I don't take offense to you wanting more in a man, as beautiful as you are, you deserve the best. I'm now currently in my last year of law school and once I pass the bar; the possibilities will be endless for me. So I'm basically begging you to look past my apron." He explains after reading my mind.

"Okay." I respond speechless.

"*Okay* as in I can have your number?" He eggs on.

"*Okay* as in I understand." I clarify.

"That's fine, I can take rejection. I thought I'd give it a shot still, you know. No basket was ever made by not shooting." He jokes.

"No, no… don't take it as rejection. I am already in a situation." I admit.

"You mean with that guy you came in here with the last time you were here?" He asks.

"Wow… you really do pay attention to me don't you?" I laugh it off.

"Yea and I noticed you both crying last time. I remember thinking to myself, that girl is too beautiful to cry."

"Yea well, like I said, I have a lot going on. Plus, you don't even know me. What if I was a mass murderer? You're just basing your perception of me off of lust." I explain.

"Not necessarily, not to be rude or anything but I see women come in and out of that hotel across the street every day. GREAT looking women, with AMAZING bodies… but I have NEVER once approached any of them. With you, with you I see way past your beauty I also see your pain, your hurt, your love, your ambition, and your fear… all when I look into your eyes."

"Wow." I am taken aback by his heart felt response, "That's beautiful and everything… but I'm pregnant. Bet you're not interested now?" I chuckle expecting his response to now be standoffish.

"That's completely fine." He responds, shocking me. "I am completely serious about courting you, this isn't lust and about sex, but about commitment, understanding, and potential love."

"Mm hmm." I doubtingly answer.

"I'm serious. It can't be all about lust anyways because as the son of a pastor, I am actually waiting until marriage to know a woman in that way." He reveals.

"Wait, wait, wait… are you telling me you're a virgin?" I laugh while nearly spitting out my orange juice.

"Yes ma'am… is that a problem?"

"No… it's just… I haven't come across a virgin my entire adult life. Not to mention I used to strip and I'm *far, far, far* from a virgin." I reiterate.

"In the words of the church… come as you are. Nobody's perfect, I don't expect my wife to be. What I do expect though is love, loyalty, and honesty in return once we get married." He continues.

"Wow. Did you just say *MARRIED*? I don't even know your name." I laugh.

"My name is Ricky and I was speaking in general, but I *am* ready for marriage. I've been so focused on school and my career… I'm actually ready for a family now." He discloses.

"Well I come with a family." I laugh as I pat on my belly.

"Again, that's fine with me." He repeats.

"Well this is awkward. You've basically just proposed to me, but you don't even know *my* name or if the man I was sitting in here crying with was my husband." I scoff.

"I already have a Master's degree in psychology. I know how to read people well. You're not wearing a ring, but that man was... I feel like he could potentially be your baby's father and even though he's indeed *A* husband—he's not *YOUR* husband. You on the other hand might have a situation of your own, but it isn't legal... and no disrespect, but whatever you have going on must not be too healthy if you were here meeting and crying with a married man." I remain silent as he tears into my life, not knowing whether to be offended or impressed. He reads my discomfort and adds, "Look, I'm not asking you to make a decision right at this moment... but here's my number." He begins to write his name and number on the back of an old receipt he had in his apron. "Call me. Today, tomorrow, next week, a month from now, hell I don't care... just call me. I'll be waiting."

"You *still* don't even know my name." I say astonished.

"I told you I ring you up almost every time you come to this coffee shop, but you've never noticed me. Today you used cash, which is unusual, but every other time you've been here you've used your card. Your bank card reads Jasmine Hall." I am dumbfounded... this guy was good... *really* good. "Listen, I just know one day you're going to want a genuinely good man in your corner, I just want a chance to be that man." He closes and then abruptly gets back to work before I can even respond. I slowly fold the paper with his number scribbled on it and carefully place it in my purse. Touché Ricky, touché.

I can't help but be reminded, in this very moment; about how Britney told me her and Jeremy met. Apparently he had given her his number at a family member's wedding, and it took her almost a year to actually use it. When Britney finally came to her senses and realized she needed a good guy in her life, she made the call and they've been inseparable ever since. I remember her distinctively telling me how she was flattered that regardless of the amount of time that had passed from the night they initially met to the time she actually used his number, he made her feel unforgettable. He remembered her as soon as he heard her voice on the other end of the phone—maybe that will happen for Ricky and I. It might be some months, years, or decades before I can actually utilize his phone number since I have way too much going on in my life right now... but what if on the day I actually use it, even if that day is in another lifetime, he is ready and waiting for me?

RING, RING my hypothetical day dream is cut short; Jeremy is calling my cell phone. I immediately come to the realization that no matter how charming Ricky the barista was, between Jeremy and Duggar, I have enough male problems to last me a million lifetimes over.

"Hello?" I pick up my phone.

"I'm here." Jeremy responds abruptly before instantly hanging up.

"Damn, hello to you too." I speak sarcastically into the deadline. I spot Jeremy's Mercedes pulling into the Vacation Inn from the window I'm sitting next to in the coffee house. I get up to leave without looking in Ricky's direction.

"No pressure!" I hear him yell after me as I walk out of the door. I blush a little to myself.

I meet Jeremy at his car. "Hi, babes!" I gallop excitedly towards him as he exits his car. Jeremy immediately puts out his arms to stop me from entering his space bubble as he gives me the kind of look that says: *Bitch! Didn't you threaten to break up my marriage and make a huge scene at my job the last time we spoke?*

"Hi." He offers up a short response.

"Yikes… you aren't still mad are you?" I giggle attempting to down play all the drama that had occurred between us.

"Look, you said you wanted to talk so I'm here. Let's just get this shit over with." He retorts.

"Yes sir!" I say mockingly while standing at attention before leading Jeremy to my room—well technically his room. He *has* been paying the tab.

After the door is closed and we are both comfortably seated apart on the bed, he wastes no time in getting straight to the point. "What do you want from me?"

"I want you to be happy." I respond swiftly.

"HOW CAN I BE WHEN YOU'RE PREGNANT? I'm happily married." He reasons.

"Are you?" I contest. "What happened to all that crying and conversation about she hurt us both? The last time we were at this hotel you were a complete wreck. She did that to you, not me!" I argue.

"I know… but I regret it. I was stupid to think I could replace hurt and lies with more hurt and lies. Jasmine, I prayed on it and I just can't do this anymore. We both have our separate situations we're dedicated to. This baby will be nothing but trouble. I don't love you." He honestly divulges. My heart immediately shatters into a million pieces. Being rejected by both the men in my life that I care the deepest for in the same week is beginning to take a toll on me emotionally. "I love Britney, flaws and all. She and I just have to undergo counseling."

"Why can't you love me flaws and all?" I respond spaced-out.

"CUT THAT SHIT OUT! YOU SAID YOU WANTED TO TALK, STOP BEING CRAZY AND HEAR ME OUT!" He responds, losing his patience.

"FUCK IT THEN, YOU LEFT ME NO CHOICE! IM TELLING YOUR WIFE!" I spew venomously.

"I knew your crazy ass would react like this, that's why I already told her." I do not expect him to say those words. I am frozen in disbelief.

"YOU'RE LYING!" I answer belligerently. He reaches in his pocket and takes out his cell phone.

"What are you doing?" I ask close to tears.

"Giving you proof that I'm not."

"Hello?" A familiar voice comes from Jeremy's phone which he's placed on speaker.

"Yea, Brit. She's here." He answers her.

"Tell that despicable bitch I know everything and that was a nice try but she needs to stay the
HELL away from me and mine or this won't end nicely for her." She menacingly discloses. *Shit*, I thought to myself, *she really did know*. I instantly feel defeated.

"I'm sorry." Jeremy chimes in after lowering his phone, "If that baby turns out to be mine after a proper DNA test has been conducted, then put me on child support. Otherwise I can't and won't have anything else to do with either of you." He instantaneously gets up to leave.

"PLEASE BABY, PLEASE!" I begin to cry hysterically and undress in an attempt to lure him back to the dark side. "You can even cum inside me again since I'm already pregnant."

"I can't, I've prayed about it and maybe you should too." Jeremy says walking away from my naked body and finally leaving the hotel room.

"FUCK ALL THE RELIGIOUS SHIT! YOU WEREN'T A PRAYING, FAMILY MAN WHEN YOU WERE ON TOP OF ME FUCKING ME RAW!" I yell after him as I get up to slam the door shut. I wasn't just going to let them get over on me; I had one more trick up my sleeve. Britney may be in the know but it's one thing to actually SEE what went down. I locate her contact information in my phone and email her the video of Jeremy and me having sex; sealing his eternal hate for me. I then drop to the floor and begin to cry myself to sleep.

"You're all I have." I repeat over and over to my unborn child as I rub my stomach and drift off into a slumber. "I guess it's just us against the world now, baby."

Chapter 16: The Return of Michael Yancy

~Present Day 2016~

I am packing up all of my belongings because it is my last day at the Vacation Inn. It seems Jeremy's graciousness has come to an end. Despite attempting to contact him for days in order to convince him to pay for a longer stay for me, I haven't heard from him. His lack of communication might have something to do with the fact that I actually sent Britney that video. What can I say? I love rubbing shit in. It wasn't enough that she knew we had been together, I wanted Britney to feel the same hurt I've been feeling. She never did respond to my email, probably too busy taking all her anger out on Jeremy.

Before I get into my car I peer into Morehouse Coffee Shop to see if Ricky is at the register... he is not. The thought of asking him to help me with a place to stay escapes my mind as quickly as it inhabits it. I have way too much pride for all that. Anyways, I can't go back to my house, for all I know Killa might be waiting there for me and I also refuse to sleep in my car while I'm this close to the train tracks. The crime in Dumois and the further west regions of Tooley isn't as bad as the crime in Chicago, but I still wouldn't feel safe sleeping alone overnight in a car; especially being a female with a body like mine and a face familiar to the locals due to having previously danced at a nearby strip club.

After racking my brain to try and figure out where I could possibly go or who I could call, I decide to call Dixie. I lie to her and tell her Duggar and I have had a huge fight and inform her that I need a place to stay for a couple of days. She insists I stay at her place for as long as I need. So after hanging up with her I begin to make my way to the Tooley Towne Apartments. The Tooley Towne Apartments are where Dixie moved after I got her a great paying job as my shop manager. Thanks to me she no longer lives in decrepit Dumois on government assistance. Even though the apartments are in Tooley, they are only two blocks away from Morehouse Coffee Shop which is located walking distance from the train tracks. This side of Tooley is still close enough to Dumois to still require much needed clean up to be considered a completely safe neighborhood. My shop is also not too far from this area, and neither is my house.

If I'm not mistaken, Jeremy and Britney used to live in the same apartments Dixie lives in now. They lived there back when we both worked at Hogan & Wildes. Now the couple lives and works hours into Tooley—that refined area is known as Uptown.

    Dixie tells me she has friends staying at her apartment helping her with rent while she is city hoping. She has resorted back to stripping since my shop burned to the ground last week. I feel a little responsible for being the reason she has to go back to that lifestyle. I really thought she had left all that behind her (especially now that we're both older), but I have enough to worry about right now than that woman's poor decision making.

    When I arrive at Dixie's apartment, I knock. As soon as the door opens an enormous smoke cloud hits me. I immediately get high from contact before I am able to get a good look at who is standing in the door way.

    "Are you going to come in or nah?" A short sarcastic ghetto girl rudely inquires.

    "I'm coming." I cough as I inhale a little more of what I gather to be weed smoke.

    "Good, cause you're letting out the antidote." She giggles. The short girl is beautiful but I am startled when I realize she is only wearing a bra. It took a while for me to notice she had no pants or panties on, but once the smoke cleared a little I saw her bare ass and slightly hairy pussy. Acting as though nothing is wrong with the scene, the short girl leads me into the living room where a strange man is seated on a coach wearing only his boxers.

    "Um… wow." I say, not meaning to actually let the words escape from my lips.

    "Don't tell me you're a square… Jasmine said you were cool." The half-naked girl laughed.

    "I'm cool, just not used to this." I respond.

    "Oh… so you never stripped?" She calls me out on my discrepancy.

    "Yes, but just not used to female nudity outside of the club if that makes sense." I answer awkwardly.

    "Okay." She chuckles as if to say I was full of shit. "I'm Sandy, that's Mark." She points at the man I had already noticed in the boxer shorts. His eyes are bloodshot red and he's taking a puff from what looks like the biggest bong I've ever seen.

"Hey." I greet them both awkwardly.

"I'm Diamond." I decide on using my stripper name. After all, when in Rome…

"Want some tree?" Mark finally speaks.

"Why the fuck not?" I decide to let loose. I needed this break from reality. I take a seat on the floor beside Mark and take several hits of his bong. Sandy and her stylish messy blonde bob and half naked petite body covered in tattoos, disappears into Dixie's kitchen and then reemerges with a tray of brownies and a bottle of liquor. *This should be an interesting next couple of days of hiding,* I think to myself.

"Want some?" Sandy giggles offering me a shot of liquor.

"No thanks, I'm actually pregnant." I reveal. "The weed I can hit since it's organic and from the earth… but I'll pass on the toxic alcohol." I justify. The next thing I know I am high out of my mind and my eyes get extremely heavy after only a couple of hits.

I wake up hours later to Sandy bent over on Dixie's couch and Mark fucking the shit out of her from the back. *Wow*, I think to myself, *they don't give a fuck!* I honestly don't even remember dozing off. My insane week along with the weed must have knocked me the hell out. Sandy and Mark having relentless sex reminded me of Killa and me in our happy days. Back when all we did was break laws together, smoke, drink and fuck… we were much less healthy together than Duggar and I. Must be nice to still be young, dumb, worry-free, and in lust. Sandy and Mark look and act no older than twenty-two.

"FUCK YES, FUCK." Sandy is screaming as she's backing her ass up on Mark's dick. She doesn't have a big butt like mine, but her petite body is beautiful to look at. Mark on the other hand is very built. From what I can tell he even has an enormous dick which he's only shoving half-way into Sandy.

"Take it, ma… come on! Be a good girl!" He coaches her.

"I can't… it's way too big." She cries back to him, her voice filled with both pain and pleasure.

"Okay… I'll go slower." He gently responds. All three of us are clearly still very high. I forgot how much better being high on weed was compared to being drunk off liquor. I haven't smoked a joint since my stripper days. I like that I don't feel nauseas right now like I would have had I been drinking. I just feel really above everything. Above my troubles, above all my fears… until not being fully coherent, I mistakenly take down a shot of liquor that was placed in front of me.

"FUCK!" I cry out which causes the couple to stop mid-stroke.

"What's wrong?" Mark asks me while the tip of his dick is still inside of Sandy.

"I told y'all I was pregnant!" I reminded to them. "I shouldn't have taken that shot that was in front of me! I'm way too high to think clearly." I whine as the couple bursts out laughing.

"Girl, I promise you nothing is going to happen to your baby, I drank, smoked weed excessively, and did crack while pregnant with mine." Sandy informs me. I am shocked, not only because her statement sounded like horrible parenting, but I had no idea she was even a mother. I wanted to ask where her baby was but I didn't really want to hold a full blown conversation with them while they were in the middle of having sex right there in front of me. "It's cigarette smoke that isn't good for pregnancies—everything else is okay. Especially weed. If everyone smoked weed, including children, the world would be a better place." She explains.

"Sure would." Mark chimes in before beginning to thrust his enormous dick back in and out of Sandy.

"OUCH!" Sandy shouts.

"Damn, you never could take my dick." He barks.

"Hey you want to come take over for me?" Sandy asks me. "Because I can't take any more of this." She admits.

"No thanks, I'm good." I chuckle awkwardly. I was good with the sex offer, and I was also good when it came to anymore weed. Regardless of Doctor *sarcasm* Sandy's opinion, I don't want to ever chance harming my baby. Also, even though Mark's girth and length are appealing, I have yet to see any condom wrappers lying around and I am *not* about that STD life.

"That's too bad… I know with an ass like yours you'd bounce on my dick like a pro." He says reading me, and he's right, I would. Getting extremely turned on by the whole conversation and the way Mark was looking at me, I get up and go into the bathroom. I lock the door and pull down my pants. I begin to rub my clit to the sex noise the couple is making close by. It takes me less than five minutes to cum. When I come out of the bathroom after cleaning myself up the two are laid out on the carpet exhausted; they both must have climaxed too. Mark reaches for his phone and hits play on a Pandora playlist.

Homeboy Duggar's - The Fakes All Around is the next song in rotation and I smile to myself. I'm glad his music is still being played even after over ten years of being absent from the rap game. Immediately when I am about to jam to the song, Mark skips it.

"Hey!" I whine. "That was my song."

"Wow, I can tell you're Dixie's friend. You two are the only two people in Tooley still fans of that fag." He laughs.

"Fag? Damn, isn't that harsh. I mean I know he's kind of a has-been, but that doesn't discredit what he's done for hip hop." I impulsively begin to defend my absentee domestic partner.

"No, don't get me wrong, I used to rock with his music heavy as well!" Mark admits.

"Look, it's not the *has-been* part that makes him a fag, it's the fact that he stays being seen with one of the biggest transsexuals in Tooley." Sandy chimes in. "I'm bisexual so I would know."

"No way!" I speak up for Duggar, "He has a live-in girlfriend. He does not fuck trannies." Of course I don't divulge that I am the live-in girlfriend I am referring to—or at least *was* the live-in girlfriend.

"No girl, he's dating a guy turned girl that used to go to my college. His name was Michael Yancy, but now she goes by Miya." Sandy reiterates. Mark plays in his phone a little before showing me a news story from an online celebrity blog. Both the picture and headline almost have me dying. It reads: MIYA, TOOLEY'S MOST POPULAR TRANSEXUAL HAS A NEW LOVE INTEREST AND YOU'LL NEVER GUESS WHO? REMEMBER HOMEBOY DUGGAR? WELL THAT'S WHO! And pictured below that headline is a recent picture of Duggar with one crutch and Miya, walking hand in hand on the street.

"Oh my GOD!" I get up abruptly, "I have to go!" I shriek as I grab all of my belongings and leave Dixie's apartment and guests without an explanation.

"That weed really got her trippin'" Mark laughs as I slam the door and run out of the apartment to my car. All I could think about was Duggar, I doubt he even knew about this scandal. We both swore off tabloids and gossip columns ever since the media began calling him a broke has-been so there is no way we would have discovered any of this. Of course Miya looked manly and strong, but I just figured she—or he—or whatever… was a strong woman. I never would have expected this if I didn't see the tabloid full of 'before and after' pictures with my own two eyes. If she could fool me, I know she has been fooling Duggar. Poor thing already has issues with his sexuality, this news might completely ruin him emotionally. I get in my car and race towards my house. I don't care if Killa is around, this was an even bigger emergency. I plan to rummage through the stuff Duggar has left at the house and see if I can find a number of Miya's to reach him at.

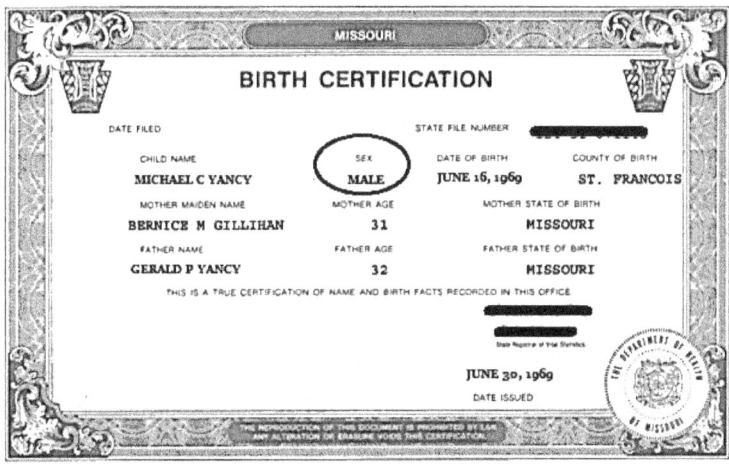

My fast-acting and worrying should not be mistaken for hate for transsexuals because I have nothing against the LGBT community. It's just that Duggar is NOT gay, and I know if he knew the truth about Miya, he would NOT accept it. Plus, I simply do not respect a woman who doesn't inform her partner that she once had a dick. With my fear of Killa overridden by my anger towards Miya, I finally arrive at my house. Fortunately, and almost miraculously, I find Miya's car in the driveway. I park right beside her, jump out of my car, and race into the house. I find Duggar and Miya packing the rest of his belongings (the one's I intended on rummaging through) into a suitcase.

"YOU ARE REALLY ABOUT TO LEAVE ME?" I ask what I already knew. Seeing that Duggar had actually come back to take the rest of his things reopened the initial wound of being left. "After EVERYTHING we've been through together? You pick— THIS over ME?" While staying at the Vacation Inn and even spending the day at Dixie's apartment, I was able to avoid the lump in my throat whenever I thought about the state of Calvin's and my relationship. We fought all the time and disrespected each other to the max, but I never in a million years would have actually expected him to leave.

"YEA HE'S LEAVING YOU FOR ME! YOU DIDN'T APPRECIATE HIM! Isn't that right baby?" An uninvited Miya jumps her way into our conversation.

"Miya, I got this." Duggar puts his hand up in her face.

"Yea, bitch, he's GOT THIS!" I reiterate.

"You chill too Jasmine; I don't want anything escalating… I just want to get my stuff and leave." He calmly explains.

"You're breaking my heart." I begin to cry. "You're really, really breaking my heart."

"How do you think my heart feels, huh?" Duggar finally begins to show some real emotion as tears stream down his own face. "YOU'RE PREGNANT WITH ANOTHER MAN'S BABY!" He wails.

"We can get through this together." I try to explain. "I know it hurts, but I'm over the guy… He really means nothing to me. I want to have this baby with you! This can be our baby to raise!"

"THAT IS NOT MY BABY!" He screams while spazzing out. "WE COULD HAVE ADOPTED IF YOU REALLY WANTED TO RAISE A BABY TOGETHER, WE COULD HAVE GONE TO SEE DOCTORS TOGETHER LIKE NORMAL COUPLES WHO CAN'T NATURALLY GET PREGNANT! BUT YOU CHEAT ON ME AND THEN YOU EXPECT ME TO STAY AND ALWAYS

LOOK INTO THE FACE OF THAT BASTARD CHILD AND BE CONSTANLY REMINDED OF YOUR DECIET?"

"That is so dumb baby; you don't ever have to deal with that kind of bullshit with me." Miya chimes in again. At this point I've lost it.

"YEA BITCH HE WON'T HAVE TO DEAL WITH THAT KIND OF STUFF WITH YOU BECAUSE YOU WERE BORN A MAN AND CAN'T HAVE BABIES!" I finally let out.

"WHAT?" Duggar is taken aback.

"She's lying." Miya snaps while turning bright red.

"I'm lying huh? Miya… as in Mi-chael Ya-ncy!" I sing while I google her name from my cell phone. "Miya, born Michael Yancy is a famous transwoman model from Missouri. She is known for her appearances in southern rap music videos and has currently been associated with former rap legend Homeboy Duggar… Should I read on?" I antagonize the couple as I show them both her Wikipedia page as proof. Duggar grabs my phone; he is clearly in a daze as he swipes up and down my screen. He slowly turns to Miya as all the blood completely drains from his face.

"Are you a man?" He finally lets out.

"Calvin, really? You should know me by now." Miya tries to calmly respond without giving an actual answer.

"ARE YOU A FUCKING MAN?" Duggar immediately lunges for her neck and begins to wrestle her to the ground.

"YOU KNEW, YOU KNEW, YOU HAD TO KNOW!" Miya exclaims, her neck tightly being squeezed by Duggar's hands. Duggar suddenly begins punching Miya in the face.

"WAIT CALVIN STOP! SHE'S NOT WORTH IT!" I jump in between them and attempt to calm Calvin's livid ass down. Miya uses the opportunity to jump up from under Duggar and run to a safe corner in the room.

"CALVIN YOU'RE STRANGLING ME NOW? FIVE MINUTES AGO YOU SAID YOU LOVED ME!" Miya cries as blood runs from her nose.

"I DIDN'T KNOW YOU WERE A MAN!" Duggar spits back.

"YOU DID KNOW, PEOPLE WOULD COME UP TO ME AND ASK FOR MY AUTOGRAPH WHEN WE WERE TOGETHER!" Miya pleads her case.

"YOU SAID YOU WERE A MODEL! God! She said she was a model... I didn't know... I didn't know..." Duggar starts to shut down, he curls into a ball and begins eerily rocking back and forth.

"I believe you baby, I know." I get down on the floor to console him. I was the only one who knew about the trauma he'd been through as a child. This moment probably took him back to the time he was assaulted and forced to suck a teenage boy's privates at eight years old.

"He knew... we had sex... he's seen me naked!" Miya continues.

"You had your dick removed Miya, you don't look that manly... I was fooled too. You should have told him; you can't go through life assuming straight men know and are okay with your sex change. Whatever you want to do with your life is your prerogative, but Duggar is not the type of man that is okay with dating a transwoman." I angrily explain.

"FUCK YOU; YOU DON'T KNOW ANYTHING ABOUT WHAT WE HAVE!" Miya snaps at me.

"GET OUT!" Duggar intercedes in my defense.

"Miya, just leave." I add.

"WHAT? You're picking me over this woman who cheats on you and disrespects you? GOT PREGNANT BY ANOTHER MAN? Holds her money and house over your head? You can't walk because of this bitch! DID YOU FORGET YOU'RE CRIPPLED BECAUSE OF JASMINE?" Miya says going into a psychotic episode. At this point I get up and walk towards her. How DARE she bring up Duggar's and my personal issues? Who the HELL did she think she was? It was about time I wiped the floors with her ass. Dragging her by her hair, I pull Miya to my front door. Eventually her wig comes off into my hand and I throw it out the door.

"Bitch, go follow your wig out of my house." I spew. Miya stands up embarrassed and attempts to cover her very low hair cut with her hands.

"DUGGAR?" She yells, a new manly bass in her voice comes out of nowhere. This is the first real sign Calvin and I are given that she used to be a man. The deep voice along with the lack of hair immediately detaches her from her feminine Miya persona allowing Michael Yancy to make his grand return. Michael looks in Duggar's direction in a final attempt at getting him to come with her but he simply looks away and ignores her. "FINE!" She finally gets the hint and stomps her way out of our home; leaving Calvin and me alone for good.

As soon as Miya/Michael is gone, I run to Calvin's side and hold him as he lets out all the tears he had been holding in. "It's okay baby… it's going to all be okay… you didn't know… I believe you. We were both fooled. It's over now; I don't care what the tabloids say… I don't care what you did with that woman… you are my king and I'm going to start treating you as such. I'm going to keep loving you unconditionally… no more other men, no more other women… just me and you… and this baby… we're going to raise it together. We're going to both get the help we need… we're going to survive this." I say rubbing away his tears and meaning every word.

"I'm sorry Jasmine, I can't believe I was so blinded by pain and dysfunction that I allowed myself to be tricked by that thing! I feel like throwing up! If I didn't have you here with me, I'd probably kill myself." Duggar cries.

"DON'T TALK LIKE THAT! We've all made mistakes! Nobody who didn't keep up with those tabloids would have known. It could have happened to anybody. We live, we learn, we grow." I advise and console my man. "But Cal, we really can't dwell on this issue. It is minor compared to what we are about to face." I inform him, changing to subject. "I have to tell you what's been going on with me since you've been gone. We are in a lot of danger, specifically me; remember I told you about Killa? Well I think he's here in Tooley and I also think he knows where we live." I add.

"SHIT! WHAT THE HELL ARE WE GOING TO DO?" Duggar sprints up, despite his injury and begins to wobble back and forth in deep thought.

"I really didn't want to bring about any fear or panic after all that drama we just had to go through, but in order for us to achieve that amazing lifestyle I just finished speaking about, I need to ensure our safety. Killa called me randomly the other night and threatened my life." I explain.

"OKAY, OKAY, SO WHAT DO WE DO?" Duggar says in a panic. He is familiar with Killa's ways thanks to all the stories I've told him, and he knows just as well as I do that Killa means business and never offers up empty threats.

"It's okay… we'll be fine… I have a plan." I inform a shaken Duggar.

"What is it?" He asks sounding a little more relaxed.

"It has to start with safeguarding our home and making booby traps… there's way too much to do right now though, so I'll explain everything on our way to the gun store. I know you hate guns, but we need to protect ourselves." Duggar nods in agreement and we immediately leave our house and hop in the car, both knowing what has to be done. Killa won't stop until I'm dead… so we have to kill him first.

Chapter 17: The Return of an Old Friend

~Present Day 2016~

    It is 3AM in the morning. Days have passed since it was revealed to Duggar and me that Miya had been born a man. We have been keeping busy taking that emotional burden off our shoulders by spending the past few days booby-trapping our house in preparation of Killa. Life is so much easier now that I don't have a shop to oversee. Thankfully my insurance company covers criminal arsons so I will be receiving a nice lump sum in the mail any day now. Duggar and I have been busy sawing traps, digging holes, and practicing our shooting—our house is now set up like a more advanced version of the home from the movie Home Alone. Our plan is to wait. When Killa shows up it will all be over for him, and whatever we do to him is going to be within our state laws of self-defense.

    Regardless of how prepared we are for the inevitable, hearing the boisterous knocking at our door at 3AM still makes the hair on both our necks stand up. We both immediately jump out of bed and give each other a knowing nod. Silently we take our posts. Duggar gets behind a telescope he built into our wall that will be able to show him, from upstairs, who is at our door.

    "What the fuck? It's a woman." He reveals.

    "What?" I abandon my post behind a machine gun and losing all fear when I peep through the telescope myself and see my other nemesis. "It's Britney." I laugh as I gallop my five-month old belly down the steps and cheerfully swing open the door. "Hello Britney, I've been expecting you— "*POW* before I am able to finish my sentence Britney punches me in my right eye. I fall to the ground way too easily, but that's only because it was so unexpected.

    "Listen you obsessed, bitch!" Britney says while she's standing over my cowardly body.

    "Jasmine, are you good?" Duggar calls from the top of the staircase. Poor thing would love to protect me but his leg prohibits him from getting to me in time. This is why we set up a lot of our traps and tools upstairs.

"Yea, everything's fine!" I yell back at him. "We're just having a friendly conversation." I add sarcastically while holding my eye.

"Like I was saying you obsessed, deranged, home wrecking, scavenger! I know you want my life, you want my husband, and now you want a family like mine but you will never be me! You and I are NOTHING alike. You are still a no good fucking scum bag stripper, and that is ALL you will EVER be. After you have that little bastard—who by the way saved you from a real ass whooping—you need to send me some DNA testing results. If—and that's a BIG if—Jeremy is the bastard's father then I will handle all the child support between the two of you. You will get a check in the mail and that's it! After this moment we want NOTHING to do with you… do I make myself clear?" Britney barks.

"Yea…" I respond defeated. I had no reason to have any dealings with Britney and Jeremy at this point especially since Duggar and I were working things. I guess Britney didn't get the memo, but right now it's 3AM and I don't have time to be arguing with her about old news when I have a killer on my tail. After I nod silently in compliance, while still on the ground by my doorway, I see Britney flip her hair and walk back to her car in her red bottoms. She definitely looks completely different since I last saw her sixteen years ago. She is way more toned and exudes a wealthy and confident aura. She has to be in her forties now… Damn, she actually reminds me a lot of our old manager and partner at Hogan & Wildes, LLP; Evica. Becoming the wicked-witch-of-the-west, Evica Wildes, was something Britney Rogers always was adamant would never happen to her, and here she was, acting JUST as stuck up as that bitch, if not more.

~Flashback 2000~

"I just want to make one thing crystal clear… Bill hired you, I didn't." A cold Evica said while glaring into my soul. It was my first one on one with her, and it occurred about a week after I started working at the firm. "I didn't get my name on the outside of this building by screwing my way to the top." She added.

"Yes ma'am." I responded. "I know Mr. Hogan has a reputation than precedes my employment at Hogan & Wildes, but I just want to make clear that I really want to be here. I really want to show you I'm here with good intentions. I've had a very rough life and I really don't want to go back to that."

"Nobody gives a fuck about your life story in corporate America, Jasmine." Evica brutally responded. "I grew up in Dumois, I lived in public housing, and I never took any handouts. I made everything possible for myself through hard work and education. Now you're a beautiful young lady, I'm not denying it... but if I so much as get a glimpse that that's the only reason you were hired... I will make your stay here a living hell." She openly admitted.

"Yes ma'am." I responded.

Of course weeks went by and Evica would catch Bill giving me the eye and observed how awkward I was around him (because at the time I was avoiding him like the plague). I knew exactly how I got the job, I just didn't want everyone to judge me and figure it out. I worked my ass off to impress Evica but all she continued to do was turn her nose up at me. On a separate occasion she made a comment about my clothes.

"What brand is that?" She scoffed.

"I can't afford brands... I get most of my work clothes from a thrift store nearby." I explained.

"Oh." She would answer rather shortly. "Well it's cute... whatever it is." She then walked away giggling. For someone who grew up right where Dixie and I lived at the time, Evica sure did put her own people down.

"Have you ever been on a plane?" Evica asked out of the blue another day.

"No... but I'm not from here, I was born in Chicago... I came here by bus." I honestly divulged.

"That's cute." She responded. I hated that bitch. Nothing was ever good enough; she was always trying to one up somebody. I noticed she did that to everyone who wasn't a top notch lawyer. Like damn, people have to start from somewhere. I used to think she harbored animosity towards me because Bill and she used to have a thing; at least that was the rumor going around the office, but I learned that's just the kind of person she was. She acted this way to delivery people, the cleaning crew, the Liberians, *even* her clients.

Britney and I would promise to never end up forty, bitter, and shallow but the woman that just punched me and walked out of my house was exactly that.

Chapter 18: Over My Dead Body Part 1

~Present Day 2016~

I wake up with a headache and a black eye curtesy of Britney Rogers. The last couple of days have put things in perspective for me. I've been in hiding for weeks and it's given me a lot to think about. I realize now I am five months pregnant and as a result, my life isn't the only life in immediate danger. I realize I've wasted the past sixteen years holding on to a stupid grudge when I could've been focusing on Duggar. I also realize I don't miss my salon one bit, hair was just a hobby, I saw it as my only means to stay afloat but I didn't love it... I basically settled. The reason I've been angry and Britney is because I wanted to be in her world and have what she has—but I no longer want that.

All I really want at this very moment is my baby's safety, Killa to go away, and Duggar and I to live happily ever after. In order to make all that happen I had to fix things with Jeremy and Britney. I pick up the phone and call Britney but she doesn't answer her phone—go figure. I decide to call Jeremy's cell phone instead.

"Jeremy Rogers, speaking." He answers his phone.

"Hey Jeremy, it's me Jasmine. Do you have a minute to talk? I'm not trying to start any drama, I just tried to call Britney but she didn't pick up her phone." I explain.

"Oh boy... here we go. Go on then, talk." He responds exasperatingly.

"Okay, you were right all along, I don't love you."

"Oh you don't do you?" He mocks me.

"No... I don't. The only reason I was so infatuated with you and your wife was because you two portrayed the image of a perfect family. I wanted that normalcy for once, I wanted a husband who loved and respected me. I saw what she had when she worked with me at the firm, and I wanted it." I cry. I am being completely honest.

"Is that all?" He coldly responds.

"No... I learned something through all of this." I expand on my views, ignoring his disdain. "I learned that you both appear beautiful and well put together on the outside but on the inside you both are just a more polished version of Duggar and I." Jeremy bursts out in sudden laughter.

"NOW THAT IS FUNNY!" He exclaims.

"No really, think about it. You both have just as many issues as Duggar and I do... Britney puts on this Christian front now, but she is from a poor and broken home and has some MAJOR daddy issues. Yes, she's rich and successful now, but back in the day she did a lot of strange for her change... Remember DC with Hogan? And you... *good boy Jeremy*... it takes two to create a baby and I didn't lie down on top of myself. I'm probably not the only woman you've fucked behind Britney's back. I don't care how much temptation I threw your way, if you were really this greatly composed man you wouldn't have knocked me up now would you have?"

"Is this why you called me? To talk shit?" He scoffed.

"No. I called you to tell you I want you and your *wife* to never contact me again. LEAVE ME ALONE OKAY! Thank you for your sperm but I no longer want anything to do with either of you sick bastards. You both need as much help as I do!"

"Oh... how nice. Well see Britney still has a lot of lawyer connects and when that baby is born we are going to get a DNA test done whether or not you agree to it. We know you're crazy and if we don't get it over with you might come back years later and try to take us for some money. This test is necessary in order to get rid of you once and for all. Once the test results come in and we find out the bastard you're carrying is not mine, we will get a restraining order against you and carry a gun with us at all times. If we so much as see or hear from you again, we'll kill you. And if—and that's a small if—that baby turns out to be mine, Britney and I will file for full custody because I think the courts will agree a former stripper surrounded by violence isn't qualified to raise a child."

"WHAT THE FUCK ARE YOU SAYING?" I scream into the phone.

"That if that baby is mine, you might as well kiss him goodbye at the hospital. No way I'm going to let your sick and twisted ass raise any child of mine." He chuckles devilishly. "You see Jasmine, you messed with the wrong family. You should have just left me alone. We don't fear you and your little bastard, but you should fear us."

"ARE YOU THREATENING TO TAKE MY CHILD?" I question him in disbelief.

"Oh so now he's *your* child, but at the hotel he was *our* baby?" Jeremy laughs.

"I used to think you were a better person. Before you fucked me you gave off an honestly good aura. I've only met one other man that has given me that kind of a feeling… and that was my father. Now I know you are NOTHING like my father. You Jeremy, are the devil himself. If you know what's best for you, your wife, your daughter, and your son Jeremy it is YOU who won't EVER contact ME again." I say before I slam the phone down.

~Flashback 1994~

The first time I had ever spoken up for myself was back when I was fifteen years old. Two months after Killa had paid my uncle an unforgettable visit that left him shaking in his boots, I began a steamy friendship with the heinous teen. Our first date was to the movies. Killa didn't speak much but he really didn't have to, at the time he was a hero in my eyes. I forget the movie we went to go watch, but I remember it involved a lot of action because Killa began to hoot and holler for the bad guy. It turned me on how backwards he was. Everyone in the theater was actually annoyed by the noise he made but they were all afraid to say anything. His reputation definitely surpassed itself.

Killa dropped me off in a brand new Lexus, mind you he was only eighteen at the time but he had a better looking car than my uncle or any other adult on my block. My Aunt Leslie nosily glared from the kitchen window as Killa walked me to my stoop.

"I had a great time." I remember him telling me.

"Me too." I blushed.

"We definitely have to get up again so make sure you stay beautiful and good for me okay?"

"Okay." I continued smiling.

"I'm serious. Stay sweet." He reiterated as he gave me my first kiss on the lips.

"I will." I swooned as I floated into my house and watched as Killa finally drove off.

"WHAT THE HELL WAS THAT?" My aunt barked as she came from the kitchen. I hadn't come home since school was let out.

"Killa picked me up from school and took me to the movies." I informed her.

"The nerve of your ass!" My aunt snapped.

"What's going on?" My Uncle Dennis said running up from the basement.

"This floozy just had Killa drop her off and now she's talking about *he picked me up from school and we went to the movies.*"

"What?" Surprisingly all the anger rushed from my uncle's face and immediately turned into fear. "You and Killa dating now?" He asked, visibly shaken.

"Yes." I boldly responded, knowing damn well that Killa put the fear of God into my uncle's heart.

"Okay then, as long as she was back by nine." My uncle calmly stated and then began to waddle back into the basement.

"WHAT?" My Aunt Leslie spat. "THAT'S IT? I was about to beat her ass."

"That's—that's not necessary." My uncle responded stuttering. At that moment I gave my aunt a devilish grin as I walked to my room.

"I think I'm going to marry the kid, her really, really likes me." I say loud enough so that both of them hear me. That was the day I realized the full power that actually came with being Killa's girl—my uncle never laid a hand on me again.

Chapter 19: Deranged

~Present Day 2016~

It's been three nights since Jeremy called me with that bullshit about him and Britney taking full custody of my baby. I've been calling Britney's cell phone non-stop wanting to have a conversation with her woman to woman. I'm scared that if Jeremy does end up being the father and this case goes to court, the judge will pull up my record and know that people around me have been dropping like flies; my parents, my uncle, my aunt, etc. I'm scared that although I haven't been found guilty for any of those crimes that the judge will still say that I provide an unfit environment to raise a child. The court system will probably look at the picture perfect relationship the Rogers have, and their already excelling children and rip my baby from my arms and hand it over to them.

It's 2AM and I am lying in bed awake replaying all the above scenarios in my head over and over again. I hear a car pull up in our driveway. I feel Duggar wake up from the same noise.

"Britney." I say to him as he rolls his eyes and turns back over to go to sleep. Duggar wants no parts in this girl fight, but he did say if she ever hit me again he would break her arms. I reassure him that he would never need to intercept because the night she hit me I was caught off guard. Now that I am aware she is fully capable of offering up a sucker punch, I will always be prepared for a one on one with her. Grabbing a bat that I lay under my side of the bed, I get up and march downstairs ready to face that self-righteous whore.

I put on my house slippers and then I unlock the front door, bat in hand, ready to rip Britney's behind to shreds if she didn't take back what her and Jeremy were planning. The car in our driveway has on high beams that are blinding me. "GET OUT OF THE CAR BITCH!" I yell while playing with the bat in my hand. I've really been waiting countless hours for this reunion.

When the car turns off and the lights go out with it, I am scared shitless when it is not Britney's face in the driver's seat staring back at me—instead it is Gary "Killa" Lewis'. He calmly gets out of the vehicle looking deranged and grinning from ear to ear.

"Is that for me?" He says referring to the bat. "You ever heard the saying don't bring a bat to a gun fight?" He then moves his oversized shirt so I am able to see the two pistols he has tucked in his waist band. I freeze in place as all the blood runs out of my body. I can't believe I am standing face to face with the boogie man. He might as well be the devil when it pertains to my life, whenever I have a nightmare, his face is in it. Killa looks completely different than what I remember, if we weren't staring each other dead in the eye, I would probably not be able to recognize him if he was across the street. I guess being in jail for eight years and then being on the run takes a toll on you. His once flawless dark skin was covered in cuts, bruises, and acne. His hair that he normally kept clean was growing wildly and left unwashed. He looked like he had lost a huge amount of weight because his face was so skinny he looked sickly, I just can't believe he was ever that handsome well put together man I once worshipped.

"Killa, please." I finally manage to say after what felt like an eternity of staring each other down. "I'm pregnant."

"Oh… wow… little Jasmine is going to be a mommy! Woopty-fucking-doo. I knew you were a whore, but what I didn't know… what surprised the fuck out of me… was that you are a killer too. You killed your uncle and your aunt and you pinned them both on me, so on top of everything you're a great liar. You lied to the police and you lied to me when you told me you were a virgin!" Killa sang. His tone was creepy as hell because it was almost melodic and seemed rehearsed. If I didn't know Killa's reputation, I would think he was joking with me and didn't really pose a huge threat—but I knew better. I knew that if I didn't run back into the house within the next three seconds, Killa would kill me and my baby with absolutely no remorse. Knowing this, I act fast and run.

As soon as I hit the doorway, I hear one of Killa's guns go off. I drop to the floor from a sharp pain in my side. I'm thinking it's from the severe stress I'm putting on the baby until I see a lot of blood coming from the side of my stomach.

"Jasmine is everything good?" I hear a panicked Duggar asking from upstairs.

"DUGGAR IT'S KILLA, NOT BRITNEY!" I scream. I hear Duggar getting in place for the trap as we practiced many times before. I scoot further into the house so that when Killa walks in after me he's an easy target for Duggar. Just as planned, Killa follows suit.

"YOU DUMB BITCH! YOU SET ME UP! NOW I'M GOING TO MAKE SURE YOU AND THAT BABY DIE SLOW!" He says putting away his gun and taking out a blade.

"Hey fuck boy! I believe the correct saying is don't bring a knife to a gun fight!" I boldly interrupt Killa's rant and point directly above his head where a barrel of a gun is looking right back down at him. *POW* Duggar immediately takes one clean shot from upstairs, blowing Killa's face off once and for all. I watch Killa's lifeless body fall to the ground as everything around me turns black and I fade away.

~*Flashback 1996*~

"Ms. Hall is it true that in the time between 1994 and late 1995 Gary *'Killa'* Lewis held you hostage *against your will* at his residence?"

"That is correct." I remember answering the prosecutor in Killa's case. He was on trial for the murder of my Uncle Dennis and I was one of the star witnesses.

"Is it true that during the time you were held captive, Killa had killed a man by the name of Thoman Fendy in your presence?"

"Yes it is." I responded again, I could feel Killa's eyes searing right through me, telepathically burning a hole through my face.

"And on the night of your uncle's death where was Killa?"

"He… he… beat me after drinking a lot and took his car keys saying he was going to go kill the man I loved the most. You see, I didn't grow up with my parents and my uncle was really all I had." I started to cry on cue. I could hear my aunt losing her own grip on reality as she began to wail from the stands as well.

"ORDER IN THE COURT!" The judge said as he banged his gavel a couple of times.

"Did you see what he did when he came back to the house that night?" The prosecutor continued to question me.

"Yes. He came home in a panic, went to the bathroom, threw off the hoodie he was wearing and said to me *I DID IT, I FINALLY OFFED YOUR UNCLE, JASMINE. I'M SORRY, BUT THAT MAN OWED ME SO MUCH MONEY FROM ALL THE DRUGS I SOLD HIM! I HAD TO DO IT*" I acted out my best Killa impersonation for the jury. Immediately after my show, Killa jumped up from his chair and started yelling at the top of his lungs.

"FUCK YOU, YOU BITCH! I'M GOING TO KILL YOU! WHEN I GET OUT OF HERE I'M GOING TO FUCKING KILL YOU! YOU DID THIS BITCH, YOU KILLED YOUR UNCLE, NOT ME! I'M GOING TO FUCKING WATCH YOU DIE SLOW!" He instantly lost his mind and became deranged.

"ORDER! ORDER!" The judge directed the policemen in the courtroom to carry Killa off to the jail. It took about six police officers to restrain him.

He has always been the scariest man I've ever known in my lifetime—my personal boogieman—and now… he was finally dead.

~Present Day 2016~

I wake up in a hospital bed. I have no idea how much time has passed.

"Britney?" Duggar and Dixie jump up from the guest chairs in the room and run to my side. "we've been worried sick about you!" He informs me.

"What happened?" I ask rather confused.

"You were shot in the stomach." Dixie cries.

"Oh my God!" I panic.

"It's okay baby, it's okay, miraculously your baby is fine." Duggar reassures me. I look down at my stomach and am still able to feel my baby moving a little bit inside of me. I lift my hospital garb and realize my stomach is wrapped up in bandages.

"The bullet missed the baby by 4 inches." Dixie added. "This really is a miracle; you've been asleep for almost a day."

"Wow… and Killa?" I ask looking at Duggar.

"He's dead." He says confirming what I already knew. "Police say he was on our property so it was self-defense. I was also told that the Missouri House approved a bill that expanded the self-defense law against home intruders. The castle doctrine law was approved in 2007. It gives Missouri residents like us the right to defend ourselves and our property. That law allows the use of deadly force for someone who is breaking into our home like Killa tried to do. It also expands to our car and even if we were renting and it wasn't our property, we'd be justified."

"Good." I say as I shut my eyes. I am exhausted and relieved that we are all safe, including my baby, and now Killa was out of our lives forever. I knew we wouldn't be charged if we killed him at our house, not only was Killa a felon on the run but he already had a history of killing off my family members. The police anticipated him coming back for me to finish the job. Duggar and I already researched and knew all that about the self-defense laws when we were putting our booby-traps together, I think he was just repeating everything more for Dixie than for us. She still doesn't know much, for all she knows the same people that shot Duggar in the leg in 2005 came back to finish the job and failed.

Chapter 20: Over My Dead Body Part 2

~Present Day 2017~

It's been four months since I was shot just inches away from my colon. Miraculously, both my baby and I survived. In fact, he was born two months ago on December 18th 2016. I named my healthy six pound, eight ounces of joy; Evus Milagro Duggar. Evus, I came up with by combining the names of my parents Eva and Cyrus. They are a perfect example of the love I want passed on to my son. Also Milagro is miracle in Spanish, and although Duggar doesn't speak any, he does have some Cuban in his blood. Not to mention this baby is the perfect example of a miracle; not only in the way he was born, but also how he brought Duggar and I closer together than ever before.

Currently, I am holding Evus now as we wait for Calvin to come home from work. Yea that's right, the day after I was omitted from the hospital; Duggar surprised me and told me he snagged a job writing jingles for businesses. I always knew he had it in him to do more with his life, even with his injuries… but it was always a pride thing for him. He didn't want to go from mega superstar to any old mundane type of worker—but when he saw Evus' face, everything changed. He helped more around the house, he found work (even if it wasn't his dream job), and he really took initiative and took control as head of our household. Killa was the first person Duggar killed and it changed him emotionally for the better. He is politer to me than he's ever been and he's made it a rule to never curse in front of our son. That's another thing… even though Duggar isn't Evus' biological father, he's stepped up and loved him as if he were his very own.

As for me, I've changed as well. Duggar and I are actually planning our wedding—I finally said yes when he asked me to marry him a week after I came home with Evus. I never thought real love could blossom from our dysfunction, but I guess when two people have something greater to live for they ultimately become way better people.

While I am breastfeeding I hear a knock at the front door. Evus is close to falling asleep anyways, so I gently place him in his crib as I go downstairs to see who it is. It's still extremely early for

Duggar to arrive home, he usually gets home at five and it's only about 1PM. (Mind you, Duggar doesn't even really need to work, the house is already paid off and there was evidence found within the last couple of months that Killa was the one who set my shop on fire. Luckily Tooley's Hair & Nails was insured so I received a nice check. I decided not to use the money on opening up another shop and just put half of it in my son's college fund while the other half I used daily).

    I open up the front door and to my surprise, standing in my doorway is Jeremy Rogers. He looks rather exhausted and I am confused because these are his work hours. Curious as to why he is at my doorstep, I invite him in.

    "How may I help you Mr. Rogers?" I say rather professionally.

    "Oh, so now it's Mr. Rogers?" He scoffs.

    "Well ever since your wife punched me in my face and you threatened to take my child away I've taken you out of my friend zone." I respond.

    "Understandable." Jeremy laughs and then clears his throat while pointing at my chest. I look down and to my dismay my swollen breast is still hanging out of my bra and over my shirt. I am a new mother so this is a common mistake I've made before.

    "Don't flatter yourself… I was breastfeeding." I say irately.

    "Congrats on the baby, I'm guessing by all the blue in your house, it's a boy?" He asks.

    "Yes. His name is Evus." I inform him.

    "Why didn't you call me?" Jeremy gets instantly serious.

    "Because there was no need to. His name is Evus Milagro Duggar, so he already has a dad."

    "That's cold." Jeremy sighs.

    "Cold world." I respond shortly.

    "Yea well… you're right. I deserve it. I've been treating you like scum lately, but I came here to make amends." He explains.

    "How?" I ask curious as to what Jeremy had in mind.

    "What time does Duggar come home?" He randomly inquires.

"Five, six at the latest." Immediately after I finish my sentence Jeremy picks me up and places me on my kitchen counter. He begins to intensely kiss along my neck, chin, and face.

"STOP!" I respond, disgusted.

"Oh come on… this is what you wanted isn't it." Jeremy gets even more aggressive and begins to squeeze my plump breasts and thighs. "Having that baby has really made you extremely thicker… I mean you were thick before, but your body now is unreal." He coos. Ignoring his advances, I hop of the counter and push him off me even harder. Jeremy is more turned on by my rejection and this time scoops me up against my will and gently places me on the kitchen floor. He pins both my arms above my head with one hand and lifts my shirt with the other. "I want some milk too." He says as he begins to tenderly suck on each one of my nipples. When I am finally able to free one of my hands I give him a good slap. Jeremy finally gets off of me.

"Are you mad? Are you crazy? I am engaged! You see this ring?" I angrily inform him, showing him my nice sized engagement ring.

"And I am married, but that didn't stop you. I finally get what you were trying to tell me at the hotel down the street. You wanted me to co-parent with you and fuck you on the side, while we both kept our respective situations. I am completely on board now." He admits.

"Yes, you're right. That's what I once wanted, but not anymore. I love Duggar and my child, and I am honestly over you and Britney. I don't want an open relationship any longer, and you made it clear you wanted her over me back then." I remind him.

"Yea, well all that was before she stopped fucking me… Since she saw that video of you and I that you maliciously sent her, she hasn't so much as touched me. I think she's only staying with me until this whole baby thing blows over because she doesn't want to lose to you. She's conniving. If you weren't initially into me, she would have thrown all my shit out on the lawn by now. Now that there's another woman, she's being extra nice as a way to kind of *keep her enemy close*. How dare that bitch try to punish me when before we got married she was fucking every man in Tooley."

"I'm not a marriage counselor." I interrupt.

"You ruined my fucking marriage, so you're going to get what you wanted!" Jeremy snaps as he begins to aggressively tug at my jeans. In a panic I scream hysterically, and out of reflex, I knee Jeremy's genitals before he is able to fully undress me. "FUCK!" He screams as he rolls off me.

"Fuck you!" I respond and go into my drawer and retrieve a kitchen knife.

"What you're going to kill me like you did that guy Killa? Everyone knows about it. Even my lawyer." Jeremy scoffs.

"Lawyer?" I ask confused.

"Yes lawyer! The one Britney and I hired. Now I was only going to come over here and get some and come to a mutual decision about the baby, but since you love playing dirty, then here." Jeremy still on the floor holding his hurt privates reaches in his pocket, pulls out and envelope and slides it over to me. I open it up and it's a court ordered paternity test. "We want full custody of my son." He spews. "He isn't safe in this crazy ass household full of killers, former strippers, and ex-rappers." He says laughing.

"GET THE HELL OUT! GET THE HELL OUT!" I scream as I kick him towards the front door. Jeremy finally getting to his feet waddles to the doorway and lets himself out.

"See you in court!" He laughs. "And wait until I tell Britney you hit me in the groin because I wouldn't fuck you when I came here to serve you with those papers!" He adds while getting into his car. "I'm sure she has another black eye with your name on it!" He yells out the window as he drives off.

"That scumbag." I say to myself. I slam the door behind him and immediately hear baby Evus crying hysterically. I run to his side, take him out of his crib and begin to breastfeed him again and rock him back to sleep. "No one is going to take you from mommy, baby, NOBODY… that'll happen over my dead body!"

Chapter 21: Britney's Revenge

~Present Day 2017~

Baby Evus and I have just come home from his six-month physical with our pediatrician. I'm so proud and happy that my joyous, chunky, healthy baby boy is developing normally and showing signs of an advanced intellect. Duggar and I can't be any prouder of our little, adorable bundle of joy. I haven't been away from his side for the entire six months. I love everything about my baby. We read to him every night just like my parents had done to me. We are going to give him the best life possible.

Anyways, while baby Evus is jumping giddily in his carrier which is hanging off the front of my shoulders, I habitually check the mailbox before entering the house. "Bills, bills, and more bills." I chant loudly to myself. I stop when I notice an envelope that seems out of the ordinary. It listed the sender as: Tooley Testing, Biometrics & DNA Center. "Oh shit." I curse under my breath. This must be the DNA test results. Do I even really need to open it? At this point I just needed to get my lawyers together because now that the proof existed that baby Evus was in fact Jeremy's son an inevitable, and intense, custody battle was just around the corner. My heart begins to hurt at the thought of losing Evus forever.

"I have a gun cocked and pointed at the back of your head, walk decisively yet quickly into the house and no one will get hurt." I hear a familiar voice barking directions from behind me—*it's Britney*.

"Come on now, I thought we were over this. I have my six-month old child with me. Please just calm down." I beg her.

"Just get in the damn house!" She snaps. Over six months ago I allowed her to get away with punching me in the eye so I'm guessing she takes that as weakness, but if only she knew I would not play any games when it came to my child. I do as she says for the time being and rapidly walk into my house, aware that Duggar is asleep upstairs from working the night shift at a second job he has recently picked up. "Put the baby in his play pen and then come back here and have a seat at the bottom of the steps." She further instructs me. I am grateful I am able to place baby Evus in a safe place and finish talking out our differences with him being out of my arms.

"Okay Britney, what is all this about? I haven't heard from you or Jeremy in a while." I begin.

"Please spare me with the dumb act." She snaps." I know you're still seeing my husband behind my back after I SPECIFICALLY told you to BACK THE FUCK OFF!"

"That, my love, is where you're mistaken! The last time I saw Jeremy was a couple of months ago when he came on to me! You both are lucky I didn't press charges. I continuously told him to stop, to leave me alone, I told him I was in a different place in my life, but he continued to unwantedly force himself on me." I explain.

"You're lying!" She says exploding into a frenzy, standing over me waving her nine millimeter in my face as I stay seated calmly on the steps.

"With all due respect, shouldn't I be the one waving that gun around after Jeremy threatened to take my child away from me? I have done nothing wrong." Just then Britney strikes me in the face with the butt of the gun causing my face to bleed.

"SHUT THE HELL UP! What you're not going to do is try to make a fool out of me!" She screams.

"I am not trying to make a fool out of you, I am stating facts! Jeremy came to me wanting to be with me almost four months after Evus was born. He didn't want to leave you, but he wanted us to continue our affair. He wanted to become a happily blended family. Now I'll admit, that's the idea that I approached him with when I first found out I was pregnant, but after I actually saw my baby, all I want to do now is the right thing. I even put Duggar on the birth certificate; I just want to live a normal life. I am focused on being a wife, and I'm getting married soon. My relationship will no longer be an open one." I clarify.

"OF COURSE YOU WOULD SAY ALL THIS SHIT AFTER YOU HAVE COMPLETELY SHATTERED MY ENTIRE MARRIAGE AND FAMILY DYNAMIC!" She snaps, this time loud enough that the noise startles my once calm baby into a hysterical episode. "JEREMY AND I DON'T EVEN SO MUCH AS LOOK AT EACH OTHER ANYMORE AND IT'S ALL YOUR

FAULT!" She lifts up her arm to strike me a second time when Duggar suddenly appears.

"CHILL OUT WITH ALL THAT IN FRONT OF MY SON!" He yells from the top of the steps. He is holding his own pistol in his hand. "YOU NEED TO LEAVE, NOW!" He adds.

"STAY OUT OF THIS YOU HAS BEEN!" Britney barks right back at him.

"This is ridiculous; I'm calling the police." Duggar says restlessly as he reaches in his pocket for his phone. In a panic Britney raises her gun away from my face and points it at Duggar who in turn raises his own gun towards her and immediately and simultaneously both guns go off.

"NO!" I scream as I run up the steps to Duggar's side. He has been shot in the chest and is stiffly lying on our grey carpet. Blood is oozing out of the hole in his chest and is soaking up the area round him. "NOOO!" I begin to cry extremely hard. Duggar is clinging to life, eyes fighting to stay open.

"911 Hello…?" I hear a muffled voice coming from the other end of Duggar's phone which is now on the floor next to his unconscious body.

"Hello." I pick up the phone. "My fiancé has been shot by an intruder. She had a gun… I don't know what to do… he's dying!" I contain myself enough to respond.

"We're sending help, just stay with him. Where is the intruder now?" That was the first time I noticed Britney's lifeless body on the ground. As I walk towards her I notice Duggar's aim had been almost perfect, the bullet went straight in between her eyes. There is no way Britney survived. "Ma'am? Where is the intruder now?" The 911 operator repeats.

"She's dead." I numbly respond.

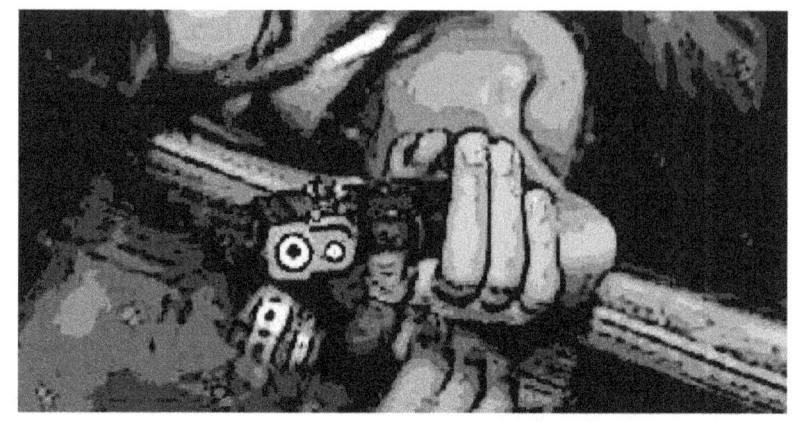

Chapter 22: Angel of Mine

~Present Day 2017~

    Britney is confirmed dead on arrival by the police and emergency crew. Even though I once hated her I was in a state of disbelief that it actually happened. Now that I was a mother, I felt an intense feeling of sympathy for her children and even for Jeremy. Britney's is the only murder I've witnessed in my entire life that I have felt bad about. Years ago this would be at the top of my wish-list, but in this moment of my life, I mourned for her as if she were my blood sister.

    There is one other person clinging to life in intensive care that I can't imagine losing as well, and that is Calvin Duggar. The love of my life, the acting father of my child, the center of my very being is holding on for dear life as I am seated right there by his side. Dixie is downstairs in a waiting room with my infant, we have been at the hospital for nearly five hours and my heart keeps breaking every time I hear a peep coming from the machines Duggar is hooked up to.

    "I... want... you... to... take... good... care... of... Evus." Duggar tries to say.

    "*Shh* baby, don't talk just get better and rest." I say as I gently plant a kiss on his forehead.

    "I... want... you... to... call... my... lawyers... when... I... die... there's... money..." He tries to talk to me about all the things I should do after he dies not understanding that his death would not be an option, not now and not for a while.

    "STOP IT RIGHT NOW! YOU FIGHT, YOU HEAR ME? YOU FIGHT!" I cry. The doctor and some nurses come in to do a routine check up on Duggar and I know it is my cue to leave the room. I go rejoin Dixie and Evus in the hospital lobby.

    "How's he doing?" She says close to tears. I forgot how much she loved and respected Duggar as a musician, so I realize even though they weren't close friends she was still connected to him in that way. This emergency situation has also actually brought out thousands of Tooley/Dumois residents who are currently surrounding the hospital, holding up signs that read things like: **GET WELL SOON, HBD** or **PULL THROUGH KING OF**

RAP! I am overwhelmed by how many people still loved him and his music, it truly touched me and I am hoping Duggar understanding he is still tremendously loved will be a reason for him to push through and recover.

I begin to cry when I see a little boy and his father with a HBD shirt outside of the door speaking to media personnel. Reaching in my purse to pull out a pack of tissue, I randomly notice the DNA test results in my bag and I don't know what makes me decide to pull it out, open it, and read it… but I do. I skim through the letter and go right to the portion where the results are listed and read:

We have now completed our calculations and based on the evidence from the DNA submitted for analysis it is our belief that Jeremy Allen Rogers (born 01/04/1973) is excluded 99.9% from the paternity of Evus Milagro Duggar (born 12/18/2016).

"Oh my God!" I yell while immediately dropping the letter.

"What's the problem?" Dixie asks in a panic, concerned about me.

"Jeremy's not the father." I say more to myself than to her.

"Who's Jeremy? Not the father of whom?" Dixie is extremely confused; ignoring her I run back up the steps to intensive care to share with Duggar the unbelievable news.

You see, if Jeremy Rogers isn't Evus' biological father there is only one other incredulous possibility of paternity—Duggar. Bursting through the doors as the nurses are caring for Duggar, I scream so he can hear me "YOU ARE EVUS' REAL FATHER! I JUST OPENED THE DNA TEST RESULTS! THEY CAME BACK NEGATIVE DUGGAR! YOU ARE EVUS' FATHER!"

"Ms. Hall, Mr. Duggar needs his rest if he's going to get better. It's currently not looking that good for him." The doctor admitted while attempting to calm me down.

"LET ME TALK TO HIM! PLEASE! I KNOW WHAT WILL GET HIM THROUGH! HE'S THE BIOLOGICAL FATHER OF MY SON! HIM KNOWING AND UNDERSTANDING THIS WILL MAKE HIM PUSH HARDER TOWARDS SURVIVING!" I argue. "PLEASE, JUST PLEASE GIVE ME FIVE MINUTES ALONE WITH HIM!" I beg.

"Okay." The doctor instructs all the hospital employees to leave the room as I rush to Duggar's side holding his hand as his eyes slowly open.

"Duggar... baby... Calvin... you're the father!" I start to cry uncontrollably. "Evus has been yours all along... can you imagine? Our baby really is yours." Calvin doesn't speak but I see a faint attempt of a smile appear on his face. "You HAVE to fight baby, ESPECIALLY NOW MORE THAN EVER! —COME ON! FIGHT!" I cry even harder.

"Take care of my son..." Duggar manages to let escape. "Make sure he knows I've loved him since the day he was born when I held him in my arms. Make... make... make sure he knows... his parents are crazy but we love him. You take care of my son... and yourself. Call my lawyers. I love you, Jasmine." Immediately after my name leaves his lips the machine beeps and Duggar flat lines.

~One Year Later 2018~

Evus and I are at Duggar's grave site. It's been exactly a year since we've lost him and a lot has changed in both of our lives. For one, the talk about contacting Duggar's lawyers wasn't in vein. Apparently he not only left us in charge of his estate, but he also left us a lot of money. He used to always say *"they're not going to let me touch my money until I'm six feet deep"* and I guess there was always some truth in that. As soon as it was reported that he passed away, his music and merchandise tripled in revenue. If only people loved him while he was alive, he wouldn't have spent nearly a decade wallowing in depression. Anyways, due to a contract Calvin signed with his record label and entertainment lawyers, every cent his estate was awarded after his death would go straight to his immediate family. Thanks to me signing him onto the birth certificate, Evus and I were his only living relatives so we were awarded over eighty million dollars.

Due to Duggar's tragic death (and just every other negative thing that has happened to our family here in Dumois), Evus and I just recently moved to Potomac, Maryland. It is a much quieter place than all the cities I have lived in in my past. Evus deserves being raised here with some sort of normalcy. Even though we moved, we decided to keep Calvin in the city he's always loved and called home; Tooley. He is buried in an amazing lot where millions of his fans come to pay their respect and also a life sized sculpture of him was put up six months ago in Dumois (right in front of the house he grew up in). Evus and I are going to make it a habit to come visit daddy once a year to celebrate his life. It melted my heart four months ago when Evus spoke his first word "Daddy."

"We miss you and love you daddy!" I say for my son to repeat.

"We mwiss yew an' wuv yew dawdy!" My enthusiastic one-year-old repeats. I put him down so he can run around in sight, and play while I leave my own heart felt message to the holder of my heart.

"Calvin, I know you can hear me, I know you're there looking down on us which is why I wanted to say this; I'm glad I met you. There is no one else in this whole wide world I would have rather spent that time with. I am honored to have created a life with you, your one and only son is doing amazingly and excelling in every way. Evus will always know how great of a father you were to him. As soon as you saw him you switched up from your depressed state and became a great father who worked two jobs, and that was before we were even certain he was really yours. God, he looks just like you now… I don't know how we could have missed it. No DNA test, he is a splitting image of you. You've protected me and you've been my therapist throughout all these years. You knew my deepest and darkest secrets but still loved me flaws and all. You will live on in my heart, and I just want you to know I love you tremendously." With that said, I pick up baby Evus and we begin to walk slowly to the car.

"Downt cwy mommy, daddy loves you." My sweet little angel comes out of nowhere and says to me, without coercion. I take my son's statement as a sign from Duggar himself. I believe he is in a better place and has heard everything I had to say.

Chapter 23: Serendipity

~Present Day 2018~

The night Evus and I return from visiting Duggar's grave I can barely contain myself. As soon as I put my baby to sleep I fall to the floor in my bedroom and begin wailing.

"What now? God… please, I'm sorry for all the wrong I've done in my life… please help me have peace and guide my future steps." I let out of nowhere. Upon Duggar's death I began to think more about a higher power, I just couldn't allow myself to believe that he and my parents were anywhere but in heaven.

I notice a random piece of paper on the floor near the corner of my bed and I crawl towards it, desperate for any sign at all. It was the receipt paper Ricky (the coffee shop barista I had met in Tooley) had scribbled his phone number on. I thought to myself, *fuck it, why not?* And I proceeded to dial the number even though it had been nearly two years since I had last seen him. The paper must have fallen out of a box while I was unpacking from the move, I took its miraculous reappearance as a sign that God wanted me to use it.

"Hello? This is Ricky." His familiar voice picks up the other end of the phone.

"Hey Ricky… This is--"

"JASMINE!" Ricky finishes my sentence. UNBELIEVABLE! There is NO WAY Ricky remembers my name from all that time back. Either he has caller ID or he must have really liked me.

"How the hell did you guess it was me?" I blurted out laughing.

"I told you I'd be waiting for you. I didn't care how long you took."

"Yea right!" I doubtfully brush off his flattery.

"I'm serious, I JUST proved it. And this is my cell phone so although your number appears, your name does not. I remember your voice distinctively… plus you forget I have a mad crush on you."

"Had." I correct him.

"HAVE!" He fires right back at me.

"Okay lover boy, I believe you. It's not like it matters anyways, I moved away." I divulge.

"Oh wow, really? Because I moved too." He surprisingly shares.

"REALLY?" I laugh.

"Yea, as soon as I finished law school I left."

"What happened to you working with Hogan at his firm?" I ask.

"I didn't want to work for that fame-driven demon. I had bigger plans for myself and my potential. I'm in DC now, passed the bar here and started my own practice." He informs me.

"WOW that's really crazy!" I laugh even harder.

"Why? What's wrong?" He asks impatiently.

"I live in Maryland now… Potomac."

"DC is to Maryland as Tooley is to Dumois, we're basically neighbors." He joins me in laughter.

"OH WOW! That's crazy!" I giggle in disbelief as well.

"Well you know this means we HAVE to at least set up a meeting once. I don't know about you but I get home sick occasionally, seeing you will probably wipe that away ASAP!"

"I agree, but I have to tell you something serious before we turn this into whatever it is we plan on turning this in to." I explain.

"Shoot." He says and then listens attentively.

"I just lost someone very dear to me, damn near my husband; my father's child; Duggar."

"Understandable, but I had no idea Duggar was your child's father I always thought it was the guy that made you cry at the coffee shop." He honestly shares.

"Yea… I thought that too… turns out my son was Duggar's. Long story—but I really did love him with all my heart."

"Yea, his passing was a big deal back home, he must've been a great man." Ricky says empathetically.

"He really was, and I'm just not ready to replace him… I might never be." I honorably inform him.

"I COMPLETELY understand, and Jasmine, I am COMPLETELY willing to move at your pace. Absolutely no pressure whatsoever, we can even remain phone friends for now until you're comfortable." He reassures me.

"Thank you." I respond as we spend the rest of the night on the phone for hours talking about our past, present, and future.

~FIN~

A Tangier Tale Publishing ©2016

www.ingramcontent.com/pod-product-compliance
Lightning Source LLC
Chambersburg PA
CBHW031355040426
42444CB00005B/297